# ON CREATIVITY

David Bohm is widely recognized for his significant contributions to the discussion on the relationship between art and science. *On Creativity* is a collection of previously unpublished or unavailable essays by Bohm, which are all related directly to the nature of creativity. Bohm not only explores the latent creativity in the human mind, but he also examines and illuminates the presence of creativity in nature and the universe at large.

A significant portion of the material draws overtly from Bohm's perceptions as a practising scientist—his notions of what underlies a paradigm shift, or how laws of nature, theories and hypotheses are perceived, rationalized and axiomatized. However, the novelty and appeal of Bohm's views of these processes is the suggestion that the work of the visual artist is remarkably similar to that of the scientist. He explores these similarities at length and goes so far as to suggest that the creative processes of the scientist and the artist are at work in every person.

The late **David Bohm** was Emeritus Professor of Physics at Birkbeck College, University of London. He was the author of many articles and books including *Thought as a System*, *On Dialogue*, *Causality and Chance in Modern Physics*, *Wholeness and the Implicate Order*, and *The Undivided Universe* (with Basil Hiley).

**Lee Nichol** is a freelance writer and editor. He is also editor of Bohm's *Thought as a System* and *On Dialogue*.

# ON CREATIVITY

*David Bohm*

*Edited by Lee Nichol*

Norma,

As one of those rare individuals
who fuses integrity, clarity, humor, and
joy, you are a perpetual inspiration.
I only wish we had more opportunity
to see one another!

Affectionately,

Lee

December 1997

London and New York

First published 1998
by Routledge
11 New Fetter Lane, London EC4P 4EE

Simultaneously published in the USA and Canada
by Routledge
29 West 35th Street, New York, NY 10001

Typeset in Palatino by Routledge
Printed and bound in Great Britain by Clays Ltd, St. Ives PLC

*British Library Cataloguing in Publication Data*
A catalogue record for this book is available from the British
Library

*Library of Congress Cataloguing in Publication Data*
On Creativity/David Bohm: edited by Lee Nichol.
Includes bibliographical references and index. 1. Creation (Literary,
artistic, etc.) 2. Creative ability in science. 3. Creation in art.
I. Nichol, Lee. II. Title.
BH301. C84B65    1998
153.3′5–dc21
97–29460
CIP

ISBN 0-415-17395-7 (hbk)
ISBN 0-415-17396-5 (pbk)

# CONTENTS

# FOREWORD

*On Creativity* surveys two decades of David Bohm's reflections on what distinguishes creative processes from those which are merely mechanical. While much of the material in the volume explores the nature of human creativity, Bohm throughout links mind to the realm of natural process, ultimately suggesting that manifestations of creativity in humankind are not merely similar to the creative processes of nature. Rather, they are of the same intrinsic nature as the creative forces in the universe at large.

The human being is thus in the unique position of perceiving the dynamism and movement of the world around him, while at the same time realizing that the means by which this perception takes place—one's own mind—is of an equivalent order of creativity, participating intimately with the world which it observes. To the extent that our perceptions of the world affect "reality"—and the evidence for this is considerable—we have a corresponding responsibility to attempt to bring into being a coherent relationship between our thought processes and the world they emerge from and interpret.

Bohm draws on a variety of sources for the formation of his views—his forty-five years as a theoretical physicist; his affinity for the visual arts, and his relationships with artists themselves; his conviction that art, science, and the religious spirit are intrinsically related; and his perennial aspiration to articulate a philosophy of mind with creativity at its heart, a philosophy that could be concretely explored in the context of daily life.

In inquiring into the nature of creativity, Bohm does not shy away from questions of beauty, truth, or "the good." Along the way, he excavates a series of western cultural dualisms—abstract and concrete, intellect and intuition, inner and outer, absolute and relative—always proposing a razor's edge of attention by way of which one might "thread the needle" of these dualisms, avoid the crystallization of any thought process or paradigm, and engage in creative perceptions for which we currently have no definitions.

In the first chapter, "On Creativity" (1968), Bohm asks, Why are scientists so interested in their work? What inspires and motivates them? In essence, he says, a scientist is interested in learning something fundamentally new, in discovering new orders of lawfulness in the world he or she perceives. This lawfulness is not appealing primarily for its formalism, or for its utility in making predictions. Rather, the appeal is in the scientist's apprehension of "a certain oneness and totality, or wholeness, constituting a kind of harmony that is felt to be beautiful."

This theme—that at its inner core, scientific inquiry is richly aesthetic—is a recurrent one throughout *On Creativity*. But it is the impulse underlying this aesthetic—the impulse *to learn*—that is the focus of this first chapter. The learning which Bohm alludes to here is not the rote learning of established facts; it is learning about something truly new. Such "newness" is not, for example, acquiring information about a culture one had not previously studied, which would most likely be a simple additive process. The learning implied here is instead that of perceiving new orders of relationship, and hinges on a sensitivity to *difference* and *similarity*.

Sensitivity to difference and similarity exhibits varying degrees of creativity or mechanicalness. If, for instance, a coin is dropped on a highly patterned carpet, a certain perception is required to distinguish the coin from the patterns. However, this perception calls on essentially mechanical processes of recollecting the pattern of the carpet without the coin on it—a *difference*—or recollecting a surface with other small metal objects on it—a *similar difference*.

At the other end of this spectrum, to illustrate "the original and revolutionary nature of a genuinely creative perception," Bohm invokes the relationship between Helen Keller and her teacher Anne Sullivan. Keller—deaf, blind, and unable to speak from birth—was considered incapable of learning anything other than the most rudimentary physical routines. However, a deep transformation occurred in her consciousness when Sullivan helped her link a series of previously unrelated experiences to the shapes *W A T E R* by scratching these shapes on Keller's palm every time she encountered water.

Eventually, Keller had a flash of insight. First, she saw the connection between her previous encounters with water, and was able to perceive their similarity and relate to them in a coherent way. Of immensely greater significance, however, was her perception of the meaning and power of a *concept*. She perceived not just that the symbol "water" could represent a collection of similar experiences, but also that *all of experience* could now be structured through the use of concepts, in an unlimited array of defined similarities and differences. She was thus able rapidly to acquire capacities for conceptual understanding and meaningful relationship that were impossible prior to her insight.

According to Bohm, such sensitivity to similarity and difference enables one to perceive new orders of structure, both in the "objective" world of nature and in the mind itself: "the order and structure of our knowledge of natural law is always evolving, by a principle similar in certain ways to that of the order and structure of nature." He goes on to suggest that both Newton and Einstein had creative insights similar to those of Helen Keller, insights resulting in entirely new conceptual structures with broad application in many fields of thought and experience— different in application from Keller's, but intrinsically similar in that they led directly to the perception of fundamentally new structure.

Bohm thus posits a hierarchy of nested orders, in which (a) similarity and difference define basic orders (for example, the arrangement of bricks in a wall); (b) the relationships amongst these orders result in new structures (the wall itself); and (c) the relationship of new structures results in comprehensive new totalities (the house built from the walls). From Bohm's perspective, the sense of wholeness and beauty we may feel in the presence of a magnificent painting, an elegant theory, the stars at night, the mind itself—underlying all of these is a similar process of order, manifesting equally in mind and nature.

Beauty, then, is not simply a matter of personal opinion, dependent primarily upon the eye of the beholder. It is the result of dynamic, evolving processes that consist of order, structure, and harmonious totalities. Consequently, Bohm suggests the need for a new language in which these processes are conceived in objective terms, asserting that their coherent interplay results in an aesthetic perception of wholeness that is not strictly subjective. Following from this perspective is Bohm's view that creativity—typically ascribed to a select group of artists, thinkers, writers, and so on—is in fact not the province of the few. He suggests that, were it not for culturally sustained "blocks," the latent creativity in each person could be expressed to a degree well beyond that generally considered possible.

One of the primary blocks to such latent creativity is what Bohm refers to as "self-sustaining" confusion in the mind, in contrast to "simple" confusion. Simple confusion is that which we experience when, for instance, we don't understand directions we are given, or when we can't find the solution to a puzzle. Self-sustaining confusion, on the other hand, occurs "when the mind is trying to escape the awareness of conflict . . . *in which one's deep intention is really to avoid perceiving the fact*, rather than to 'sort it out' and make it clear." Bohm points out that this process creates an order all its own: a reflexive state of dullness in which the natural agility of the mind is replaced with torpor on the one hand, mechanical and meaningless fantasies on the other. Unfortunately, says Bohm, this has come to be considered a normal state of mind, and is therefore endemic in our culture.

Consequently, we need to give patient, sustained attention to the activity of confusion, rather than attempting to promote creativity directly. For Bohm, giving simple attention—a "finer, faster process" than confusion—is itself the primary creative act. From such attention "Originality and creativity begin to emerge, not as something that is the result of an effort to achieve a planned and formulated goal, but rather, as the by-product of a mind that is coming to a more nearly normal order of operation."

The second chapter, "On the Relationships of Science and Art" (1968), elaborates on themes raised in the first chapter: the nature of structure, the perception of fundamentally new forms, the formal properties of beauty—and raises new ones: the meaning of "truth" in science, art, and daily life; the breakdown of a "correspondence" view of reality in both science and modern art; and the cross-disciplinary implications of paradigm alterations.

Bohm frames this exploration in the context of early humanity, at a time when conscious experience likely entered rapid spurts of growth. At such a time, man would have had an increasing need to assimilate his experiences of a vast and awesome universe—a need to make sense of and relate to this universe, rather than simply react to it. In these circumstances, the underlying impulses that we now pursue separately as science, art, and religion would likely have been one unified movement of perception and response to the surrounding world. This underlying relatedness still exists, says Bohm, but requires attention and inquiry in a manner fruitful for modern times.

Such relatedness is indicated in the broad meanings of the word "true." In one sense, truth means that which corresponds to facts: One can rightly say, "It is true that the sun has risen every day for the past week." More broadly, truth means "true to itself," as in a "true line" or a "true man," indicating unbrokenness and integrity. Bohm points out that a demand for this coherent wholeness—in which factual correspondence is a necessary but not sufficient criterion—is central to the formation of theory in science. In such formation, other criteria—simplicity, elegance, symmetry—play an equal or greater role than correspondence. In this way, the larger aesthetic considerations of science are closely related to those of the artist. Though the artist works in the domain of perceptible media, and the scientist proceeds with instruments and theoretical abstractions, the inner intent and impulse of each is strikingly similar—to ascertain and manifest a certain quality of coherent "truth."

There is, however, an even deeper relationship between art and science than what is suggested by this notion of truth, a relationship that is grounded in the very fabric of experience. To illustrate this deeper connection, Bohm first points to the gradual recognition that scientific theories do not reflect an objectively certifiable world. Rather, it is increasingly understood that "each theory and each instrument selects certain aspects of a world that is infinite, both qualitatively and quantitatively, in its totality." In addition, at atomic and sub-atomic levels, quantum theory indicates "the inseparability of the observing instrument from that which is to be observed": the observing process actively affects that which is being observed, generating a conundrum of meaning that makes it ever more difficult to assume that any description objectively corresponds with "reality." The net result, says Bohm, is the realization that science cannot provide "simple reflections of the world as it is."

What science does provide are *paradigms*—"simplified but typical examples" that abstract relevant features of the world, giving insight into "the essential relationships that are significant for observation and experiment." These paradigms—operating pervasively throughout the community of scientists—become working models that serve to orient and organize data, interpretation, and the formulation of theory.

While Bohm's usage of the term "paradigm" is consistent with that of Thomas Kuhn, as expressed in the latter's *The Structure of Scientific Revolutions*, Bohm gives the term a radical slant, emphasizing the process of paradigm formation at two levels—the individual as well as the collective. For Bohm, the creation of paradigm structures is as much a phenomenological process—a dynamic internal activity that occurs prior to the threshold of conscious experience—as it is the result of meticulously collected data and consensual interpretation. In this way, paradigm formation can be seen as an individual, moment-to-moment construction—*and therefore not necessarily determined by prevailing orthodoxy*. To engage in a "paradigm shift," then, is sensorial and immediate, as well as epistemological and historical. It is this broadened definition of paradigm that enables Bohm to draw parallels between the "non-representational" aspects of twentieth-century physics and the perspective of non-representational art.

Beginning perhaps with Monet in late nineteenth-century France, the subject matter of classical painting underwent radical changes, culminating in what is now referred to as "modern art," or, perhaps more accurately, "abstraction." Though this process has had a long and varied evolution, its central thrust, in which the perceptual and intuitive processes of the painter compete with "objective" reality for display on the canvas, remains vital even today.

Bohm suggests that while any painting is in a sense abstract—even Rembrandt's portraits emphasize certain features at the expense of others—it is the particular orientation of twentieth-century abstraction that reveals a likeness to the work of physicists and mathematicians. Cubism, a defining force in the evolution of abstraction, presents radically abstracted images of the known world, yet retains components that anchor any given work in reality as we typically think of it. But in the work of Piet Mondrian, Kasimir Malevich, and Vasily Kandinsky, any recognizable reference to that known world—a body, a tree, a building—disappears, to be replaced by purely abstract or "structural" images. Such images often rely for their meaning only on what is *immediately presented*: they are considered complete creations in and of themselves, by virtue of their own inherent structure, without associative references of any kind.

Bohm's view, drawn from personal experience, is that engagement with such abstract structural works can enable the mind to perceive freshly: the creation or viewing of these works requires an active process of distilling perception and experience to their essences, implicitly allowing one to reconsider the nature of perceptual experience itself—from the ground up, as it were. To experiment in this way with the formation of new structures is thus seen as a creative act, in part because it suspends the constraints of both personal and historical conditioning, thereby enabling one to acquire a new perspective.

Bohm suggests that a similar creative process is at work in the formation of theory in science. Here it is not sufficient to perform repetitions of the same underlying conceptual base (just as it is not sufficient to produce endless artistic variations of the same theme), but, rather, it is necessary to strive for fundamentally new perceptions and formulations, however radically they may alter existing paradigms. In one sense, it is just this that science does so well.

At the same time, the formulation of theory can easily fall into excessive conservatism, thereby inhibiting the development of new perspectives. It is here, claims Bohm, that science may perhaps learn from the perceptual milieu of abstract art. For while abstraction may have rejected representation in content, it is nonetheless a medium that works in perceptible space, light, color, and form. Indeed, one of the primary functions of such works of art is to provoke a new sensibility of perception itself. Bohm suggests that such a renewed sensibility can enable the scientist to return to the very core of his or her endeavor—the rigorous observation of the phenomenal world.

Such cross-disciplinary learning, however, is not available only to the scientist. Bohm suggests that artists would do well to explore "an unbiased objective approach to structure," using the spirit, if not the precise methods, of scientific rigor to determine the wholeness and integrity of their work. He asserts that any particular artistic composition possesses varying degrees of inherent wholeness, which, while not algorithmic, are also neither random nor accidental. Consequently, the artist may bring to bear a certain objectivity when assessing his or her work for its coherence, harmony, and beauty.

A further assessment of the relationships between imagination, rationality, and intelligence comprises chapter three, "The Range of Imagination" (1976). Here Bohm outlines a four-faceted unfolding of perception in which intuitive apprehensions of new orders of reality are augmented by the clarity and precision of reason and logic. In addition, he inquires into the nature of the "intelligence" that he sees as the foundation of these various perceptual qualities.

Bohm's model posits two interpenetrating activities of mind—*imaginative and rational insight* and *imaginative and rational fancy*. In an *imaginative insight* one would literally apprehend images of a new and creative nature. An example would be the manner in which Isaac Newton resolved the contradictions in the medieval distinction between heavenly and earthly matter. In the medieval view, stars, planets, and other heavenly bodies were assumed to obey different laws from bodies on earth, which were bound by gravity. The theory of epicycles sustained the logic of the heavenly view up to a point, but eventually it became ponderously complex, and for Newton, unsatisfactory. Such questions as "Why don't heavenly bodies fall?" consequently took on renewed relevance.

While contemplating these questions, Newton had a flash of understanding, in which, according to Bohm, he apprehended "a new *kind* of image." Specifically, he had an image in which the moon *was* falling. This new image was complete, thorough, total—an imaginative insight which in essence was neither associative nor deductive.

From such an initial image, says Bohm, the mind will "unfold" to itself the basic features implicit in the insight, discerning essential relationships and meanings, or *ratios*. In Newton's case, the verbal expression of these ratios would be: "As the successive positions of the falling apple are related, so are those of the moon, and so are those of any falling material object." While the immediate totality of these relationships is what comprises the initial insight, it is the coherent explication of the ratios into objectively discernible form that constitutes *rational insight*. Here, the intrinsic meaning of the insight is tentatively formulated in a way that can be reflected upon internally, as well as provisionally communicated with others.

But to carry his insight into the domain of verifiability, says Bohm, Newton would have engaged in a process of a very different order from that occurring in the original insight and its initial explication. It is likely, Bohm claims, that in trying to account objectively for the odd way in which the moon "falls" (it never falls *on to* anything!), Newton made associative links with the existing body of scientific knowledge. Specifically, he may have considered that gravitational energy behaves in a way similar to that of radiant light energy—that it decreases as a function of distance. In part through this kind of associative link, says Bohm, precise hypotheses emerge, through which various aspects of the original insight can be tested. This associative process, and the hypotheses that emerge from it, are what Bohm refers to as *imaginative fancy*.

To the extent that the original insight has established itself via tested hypotheses, it is natural for new lines of conjecture, reasoning, and logic to emerge which build upon the basic theory. The development of this reasoning is what Bohm calls *rational fancy*. An extreme form of rational fancy occurs in the axiomatization of a theory. As axioms are developed—be they mathematical or verbal—their strict formality and compression may serve to expose hidden contradictions or limitations in the theory, indicating the need for new insights of a fundamental nature. Thus, a cycle of complementarity is engendered in which insight and fancy give rise to one another. Conversely, the formality of the axioms may encourage a rigidity of thought in which the axioms themselves—and the necessarily limited reality they convey—are taken as a kind of final truth. When such reification occurs, Bohm suggests, genuine inquiry comes to an end, and the likelihood of new insights is significantly diminished.

We are presented, then, with a map of the processes of insight which consists of four distinguishable aspects—imaginative insight, rational insight, imaginative fancy, and rational fancy. For Bohm these aspects are ultimately unified; though from one vantage point they are qualitatively hierarchical, from another they are integral and mutually informative. Moreover, the unfolding of these processes is both an individual phenomenon and a socio-historical one: individual insights "echo" through time, engendering massive bodies of theory which impact society as a whole.

However, the potential for any individual or society to manifest this fourfold dynamic process is inhibited by the collective acclimation to a more pervasive, archaic mental pattern, referred to by Bohm as *reactive/reflective thought*. Reactive thought is that which establishes reliable patterns and regularities in experience.

Steeped in primitive roots that hark back to man's early awareness of the recurrence of day and night or seasonal cycles,
reactive thought establishes a kind of bedrock equilibrium that is
central to every aspect of our experience. The carrying out of
many activities that require little or no conscious attention—the
formation of a chord on a piano, the instantaneous retrieval of a
mathematical concept, the act of dressing in the morning—are
variants of the practiced repetition of reactive thought.

As long as the environment in which reactive thought operates remains stable, this thought is functionally sufficient. But
when there is an anomaly in the environment (for instance, a
child being burned when reaching out to touch a flame), a new
process—reflective thought—is set in motion. The function of
reflective thought, which involves the whole of the nervous
system in an *imaging* process, is to accommodate the anomaly,
reorient the pattern of reactive thought, and re-establish homeo-
static equilibrium. In this respect, reflective thought is of a higher
order than reactive thought, and is disposed toward a relatively
higher degree of learning.

But the conservative power of reactive thought has the inex-
orable effect of orienting reflective thought toward its own
demands for repetition and predictability. In this way the potentially higher-order learning of reflective thought is drawn into
mechanical closure, albeit at a more functionally sophisticated
level—a classic case of putting the cart before the horse.
Consequently, asserts Bohm, reactive/reflective thought together
become a structurally closed system with unlimited content.
Only a process of yet higher order can keep this system open in a
deep structural sense. It is this higher-order process that Bohm
refers to as *intelligence*.

One salient aspect of this intelligence is that its perceptual
field is free of conditioning by any of the established patterns of
reactive/reflective thought. Such a quality of mind is able to
discern the presence of functional or oppositional categories
within the whole of its operations, and *thus determine the relevance
or irrelevance of these categories*, at any given moment. In this way,
says Bohm, the mind is kept free of the subtle domination of an
"either/or" logic that steers perception and experience into
mechanical reflexivity.

The fourth chapter, "The Art of Perceiving Movement" (1971),
is an overview of Bohm's consideration of the fragmentary
nature of thought, and the projections of such thought into the

realm of natural process. The essay outlines the manner in which attention to the movement and structure of this thought—as well as attention to the actual movement of the natural world—can together indicate a provisionally new "world view." This view, says Bohm, is consistent with discoveries in twentieth-century physics, as well as with fundamental aspects of human experience. He refers to this view as *artamovement*, in which "fitting" in all respects is paramount.

Bohm suggests that at the core of thought's fragmentation is an unconscious separation between thought's *content* and its *function*. This separation is rooted in our prevailing belief that thoughts are vaporous and ephemeral, without any real substance of their own. In actuality, however, thoughts engender automatic chains of psychological, emotional, and physiological responses which have immensely real impact within the mind, body, and society at large. For example, the thought "I must be an important person" will likely set in motion a number of motivations, energy patterns, and thought patterns, all coordinating with—or conflicting with—those of the larger culture. It is this activity, whether beneficial or destructive, that Bohm refers to as thought's *function*, as compared to any particular content.

Full consideration of the actual reality of thought must include the totality of these actions engendered by thought, as well as the artifacts and technologies that flow from thought. At the most comprehensive level, says Bohm, the whole of thought is self-replicating—it "copies" itself at the socio-historical level, transmitting useful practical knowledge as well as deeply flawed conceptions and meanings, including those of its own operation.

One problematic aspect of thought's replication is the manner in which we formulate and hold to "world views." According to Bohm, we tacitly assume that our world views are comprehensive and true, lacking perhaps only minor details; this assumption prevails in society in general, as well as in the community of scientists. Particularly within the latter, Bohm suggests, there is an impetus toward the discovery of "absolute truth." However, this impetus reflects a preoccupation with the *content* of any particular view, giving little or no attention to the view's proper *function*. According to Bohm, this proper function is "to help organize man's ever-changing knowledge and experience in a coherent way," not to solidify or reify any given body of knowledge.

One example of such a solidified view is the presumption in

physics that the universe is ultimately composed of particles. Bohm suggests that this view has repeatedly demonstrated its practical usefulness, and is clearly "true" within a limited domain. But while both relativity and quantum theory indicate the necessary emergence of a "non-particle" world view, the particle view remains firmly in place. Bohm stresses that the tenacity of the particle view need not be problematic, if an active comprehension of the *function* of views is regarded as important. In such a context, the particle view would find expression and usefulness in a limited domain, readily giving way to new views as circumstance required. But as the crucial relationship between the content and function of world views is currently not given adequate attention, the inclination to seize upon the content of "view X" as absolute truth remains strong.

In attempting to illustrate how the function of a view might properly direct the content, Bohm puts forward the outlines of a new world view. One aspect of this view, drawing from relativity theory, is that "unbroken and undivided movement is taken as a primary notion" in how we see the world. Here, all "things" are understood as limited abstractions: "Atoms, electrons, protons, tables, chairs, human beings, planets, galaxies are then to be regarded as abstractions from the whole movement and are to be described in terms of order, structure, and form in the movement." Another aspect, drawing from quantum theory, suggests that "in a deep enough view, *we in our act of observation are like that which we observe*: relatively constant patterns abstracted from the universal field movement, and thus merging ultimately with all other patterns that can be abstracted from this movement."

In the context of such an emerging view, Bohm proposes that the underlying relationships between art, mathematics, and science can be understood in a new light. The etymologies of these various words indicate a similarity in their original intent: "art" originally meant "to fit"; "science" originally meant "to know"; "mathematics" originally meant "to know" or "to learn." In Bohm's view, all of these facets coalesce in the original meaning of *good*: "gather," "together," "to join," and, by extension, "fitting together." In this way Bohm arrives at a working definition of "the good" that is not fraught with moral injunction, but, rather, is concerned with the coherent functioning of the human being, and consistent with the implications of contemporary physics.

Thus, three interrelated factors—unbroken and undivided

movement in nature, the inseparability of human experience from that movement, and the use of artistic and scientific sensibilities to discern the ever-changing meaning of "fitting" and "the good" within that movement—together constitute the basis for the world view Bohm calls *artamovement*. But like any other view that says something about the way all things are, *artamovement* is a metaphysical perspective. If one is to inquire into such a view, it is therefore useful from the start to clarify the meaning of "metaphysical."

The essence of metaphysical thought, says Bohm, is the tacit formulation "*all* is X." Yet while this formulation is apparently simple, all cultures define their sense of reality through some version of it. Just as early Greek forms of such thought—*all* is fire; *all* is flux; *all* is atoms—variously informed the manner in which that culture understood itself, so we today unconsciously practice metaphysics through our prevailing world view: *All* is parts; *all* is fragmentation.

Further, as the thought "I need to be an important person" will provide the concrete motive energy for individual action, so our present metaphysical views will dictate collective perceptions of fragmentation, and the patterns of energy and action that accompany such perceptions. But when the deep implications of "all" are at stake, this motive energy is proportionately amplified, creating a collective form of habitual thinking that is enormously difficult to penetrate. And, in fact, these two levels of motive energy fuse: The notion of individual identity—a "self"—is reinforced by the prevailing metaphysics of fragmentation, and the metaphysics is in turn certified by the concrete experience of "self" and "other."

A critical question then arises: How can we know if our metaphysical views are true or false? Given that it is folly to presume that the content of any world view—including *artamovement*—is "the truth," Bohm proposes a distinction between "truth in content" and "truth in function."

As suggested previously, truth in content relies on observable correspondence: "It is true that the sun has risen every day for the past week." But when our views are about "all that is," such demonstrable correspondence is impossible. Consequently Bohm invokes another derivation of "true," one which indicates "honesty" or "faithfulness." It is here, says Bohm, that we can glean the meaning of truth in function: to be rigorously honest about the accuracy, meaning, and implications of any content, even if this threatens our sense of security. Thus, when someone—perhaps a politician—makes a series of relatively true statements, but with hidden or "unfaithful" ends in view, he is contravening "truth in function." Yet while such activity at the political level is highly visible and transparent, and generally ridiculed, it is not in essence different from the pervasive metaphysics we all participate in each day.

However, says Bohm, if we can seriously question the need to hold rigidly to the content of any view, we may then begin to regard the *function* of our metaphysical propositions "as an art form, resembling poetry in some ways and mathematics in others, rather than as an attempt to say something true about reality as a whole."

"Art, Dialogue, and the Implicate Order" (1989), Bohm's conversation with the Danish artist Louwrien Wijers, summarizes his reflections on the nature of creativity toward the end of his life. Given particular emphasis is the manner in which his notion of the implicate order is related to art in both its strict and its broad senses, to global economics, and to his vision of dialogue.

Bohm indicates that his dissatisfaction with the largely abstract and statistical nature of the Copenhagen interpretation of quantum mechanics inspired him to seek an alternate view, one that in some way retained a connection with the world of everyday experience. This led him to suggest that the underlying mathematics of quantum theory imply "a movement in which everything, any particular element of space, may have a field which unfolds into the whole, and the whole enfolds it [the field] in it." The best analogy for this process, says Bohm, is a hologram. In a normal photograph, there is a point-to-point correspondence between the object and the image. But in a hologram "the entire object is contained in each region of the hologram, enfolded by a pattern of waves, which can then be unfolded by shining light through it."

At such an enfolded, or *implicate* level—there is an unbroken, internal relatedness of all things that appear as separate and relatively independent in the unfolded, or *explicate* order. This relatedness Bohm refers to as *mutual participation*, contending that no aspect of reality is exempt from such participation. Our everyday experience of consciousness is one immediate display of the implicate order—thoughts and perceptions emerge, create actions, and leave traces in the world, and are then folded back into consciousness, only to recur in another context or another form, individually and collectively.

This mutual participation, as manifested in the collective consciousness of humankind, is the basis for Bohm's vision of *dialogue*. The intention of dialogue is to expose the relatedness of our thought processes, and the manner in which we collectively generate fragmented realities through those thought processes. Bohm sees thought as intimately participating in our constructions of reality, while at the same time, in an act of sleight of hand, pretending that it doesn't do so. The result is rigid views perceived as deep truths—a volatile combination which may nonetheless be disentangled through the sustained attention called for in the dialogue.

But the inquiry into mutual participation extends to every area of human endeavor, including economics, where, Bohm claims it is necessary to grasp the fact that "our substance comes from the earth and goes back into it," and to perceive that "the earth is one household," rather than an array of independent economic units. Additionally, Impressionist and abstract art offer the possibility of "new modes of perception, through the senses, and new forms of imagination," which Bohm indicates are directly related to the implicate order.

Art and creativity, however, must not be restricted to any particular discipline. Indeed, suggests Bohm, history indicates that a failure to understand that creativity is essential to the whole of life can lead to a "mechanical, repetitious order" in society at large. Consequently, any given culture (including our own) may disintegrate, not only because of external forces and pressures, but also due to the "internal decay" that accompanies the dissipation of the creative impulse.

While the issues Bohm raises throughout *On Creativity* are at times abstract, his aim is practical: the regeneration of culture, as alluded to in the Wijers interview. As envisioned by Bohm, laying the foundation for this regeneration requires a rather subtle balancing act. At any given point in time we must invest ourselves in *some* view, based on the best experience and information we have at hand. To do otherwise requires a relinquishment of discernment, sensitivity, and common sense. But this investment need not inhibit the development of a creative awareness of the ever-shifting realities around and within us. It need not crystallize into absolute views, whether personal or collective, that subsist on their own projections and refuse to take into account that which is *new*.

Holding a view, and at the same time being aware of its living, transient quality, is not easy. We actually do not know how to do this. The pivotal question is, does this possibility in some way strike a chord in us? If so, we can explore this uncharted terrain, which is neither relative nor absolute. In this exploration, we might experiment with *artamovement*, or the perspective of dialogue. Or perhaps we will employ yet another provisional view, rooted in our own perceptions and understandings, creating a path while walking.

Lee Nichol
Albuquerque, New Mexico
March 1997

# ACKNOWLEDGEMENTS

Many thanks to Adrian Driscoll, philosophy editor at Routledge, for his commitment to publishing David Bohm's work; to Tim Falk at Sun Graphics in Albuquerque for the reconstructed line drawing of Ensor Holiday's original artwork; to Arleta Griffor for researching original materials; to Carol Hegedus and the Fetzer Institute for supporting forums around the implications of Bohm's work; to Basil Hiley for responding to various inquiries; to Bill Nichol for support all round; and to Norma Smith of University Microfilms International for her assistance in copyrighting, safe-storing, and distributing various materials.

Special thanks to Sarah Bohm, for her sensitive determination in seeing through this and other projects concerning David Bohm's work; and to Fritz Wilhelm, who, by collecting much of this material in years past, is largely responsible for the existence of this book.

Thanks as well to the following:

- Faber & Faber for permission to reprint "On the Relationships of Science and Art," originally published in *DATA—Directions in Art, Theory, and Aesthetics* (1968);
- MIT Press for permission to reprint "On Creativity," originally published in *Leonardo* magazine, vol. 1 (1968);
- University Press of New England for permission to reprint "The Range of Imagination," originally published in *Evolution of Consciousness* (Wesleyan University Press, 1976) under the title "Imagination, Fancy, Insight, and Reason in the Process of Thought";
- Louwrien Wijers for permission to reprint her interview with David Bohm, originally published in *Art Meets Science and*

*Spirituality in a Changing Economy*. The original event of which the interview was a part is available on video (ISBN 1–57180–261) and in print (ISBN 90–12–06619–0).

# 1

# ON CREATIVITY

Creativity is, in my view, something that it is impossible to define in words. How, then, can we talk about it? Words can indicate or point to something in the minds of the readers that may be similar to what is in the mind of the writer. I would like, thus, to indicate to the reader what creativity means to me. If you will read in this spirit, you can then see whether, and to what extent, my notions make sense to you.

I am a scientist. I shall, therefore, try to begin in this field and extend out to others. The basic question that I should like to consider is this: Why are scientists in many cases so deeply interested in their work? Is it merely because it is useful? It is only necessary to talk to such scientists to discover that the utilitarian possibilities of their work are generally of secondary interest to them. Something else is primary. What is it?

Could it be that a scientist deeply wants to discover the laws of nature, so that he can *predict* natural phenomena, and thus enable man to participate intelligently in nature's processes so as to produce results that he desires? Of course, such prediction and intelligent participation can sometimes be very interesting. But this is only in a context in which these activities are determined by something else that is more deeply significant, such as, for example, a common goal of great importance. Generally speaking, however, there is hardly ever such a common goal. Indeed, in most cases, the content of what the research scientist predicts is *in itself* actually rather trivial (the precise paths of particles, the precise number of instruments that will register a certain phenomenon, and so forth). Unless there were something beyond this that could give it significance, this activity would be petty and, indeed, even childish.

Is it then that the scientist likes to solve puzzles? Does he

1

want to get a "kick" out of meeting the challenge of explaining a natural process, by showing how it works? Of course, a scientist may often find this aspect of his work enjoyable. Nevertheless, such enjoyment has properly to come as a *by-product* of something else that goes much deeper than this. Indeed, if a scientist worked *mainly* in order to get hold of such pleasures and continue them as long as possible, his activity would be not only rather meaningless and trivial, but also contrary to what is needed for carrying out his research effectively. For the recognition that one's ideas are false or on the wrong track (which is often crucial for making real progress) generally gives rise to extremely unpleasant feelings of disappointment and failure: and to avoid these, the scientist whose *first* aim was pleasure would tend to overlook weak points in his work (as indeed does unfortunately tend to happen with surprising frequency).

It seems, then, that the answer to the question of why the scientists are so deeply interested in their work is not to be found on such a superficial level. Scientists are seeking something that is much more significant to them than pleasure. One aspect of what this something might be can be indicated by noting that the search is ultimately aimed at the discovery of something *new* that had previously been *unknown*. But, of course, it is not merely the novel experience of working on something different and out of the ordinary that the scientist wants—this would indeed be little more than another kind of "kick." Rather, what he is really seeking is to learn something new that has a certain fundamental kind of significance: a hitherto unknown lawfulness in the order of nature, which exhibits *unity* in a *broad range* of phenomena. Thus, he wishes to find in the reality in which he lives a certain oneness and totality, or wholeness, constituting a kind of *harmony* that is felt to be beautiful. In this respect, the scientist is perhaps not basically different from the artist, the architect, the musical composer, etc., who all want to *create* this sort of thing in their work.

To be sure, the scientist emphasizes the aspect of *discovering* oneness and totality in nature. For this reason, the fact that his work can also be creative is often overlooked. But in order to discover oneness and totality, the scientist has to create the new overall structures of ideas which are needed to express the harmony and beauty that can be found in nature. Likewise, he has to create the sensitive instruments which aid perception and thus make possible both the testing of new ideas for their truth or falsity, and the disclosure of new and unexpected kinds of facts.

So now we have seen that the artist, the musical composer, the architect, the scientist all feel a fundamental need to discover and create something new that is whole and total, harmonious and beautiful. Few ever get a chance to try to do this, and even fewer actually manage to do it. Yet, deep down, it is probably what very large numbers of people in all walks of life are seeking when they attempt to escape the daily humdrum routine by engaging in every kind of entertainment, excitement, stimulation, change of occupation, and so forth, through which they ineffectively try to compensate for the unsatisfying narrowness and mechanicalness of their lives.

Is creativity, then, something that is appropriate only to a few people of special talents, who rise to a level that is commonly called "genius"? Clearly, it is not *all* a matter of special talent. For there are a tremendous number of highly talented people who remain mediocre. Thus, there must have been a considerable body of scientists who were better at mathematics and knew more physics than Einstein did. The difference was that Einstein had a certain quality of *originality*.

But what is this quality of originality? It is very hard to define or specify. Indeed, to define originality would in itself be a contradiction, since whatever action can be defined in this way must evidently henceforth be unoriginal. Perhaps, then, it will be best to hint at it obliquely and by indirection, rather than to try and assert positively what it is.

One prerequisite for originality is clearly that a person shall not be inclined to impose his preconceptions on the fact as he sees it. Rather, he must be able to learn something new, even if this means that the ideas and notions that are comfortable or dear to him may be overturned.

But the ability to learn in this way is a principle common to the whole of humanity. Thus, it is well known that a child learns to walk, to talk, and to know his way around the world just by *trying something out and seeing what happens*, then modifying what he does (or thinks) in accordance with what has actually happened. In this way, he spends his first few years in a wonderfully creative way, discovering all sorts of things that are new to him, and this leads people to look back on childhood as a kind of lost paradise. As the child grows older, however, learning takes on a narrower meaning. In school, he learns by repetition to accumulate knowledge, so as to please the teacher and pass examinations. At work, he learns in a similar way, so as to make a living, or for some other utilitarian purpose, and not mainly for the love of the action of learning itself. So his ability to see something new and original gradually dies away. And without it there is evidently no ground from which anything can grow.

It is impossible to overemphasize the significance of this kind of learning in every phase of life, and the importance of giving the action of learning itself top priority, ahead of the specific content of what is to be learned. For the action of learning is the essence of real perception, in the sense that without it a person is unable to see, in any new situation, what is a fact and what is not.

Of course, there is a routine and mechanical kind of perception that we can carry out habitually, in dealing with what is familiar. This is generally what we tend to do (for instance, few people ever note more than a small number of habitually determined salient features of their friends, of the places in which they live, and so on). But real perception that is capable of seeing something new and unfamiliar requires that one be attentive, alert, aware, and sensitive. In this frame of mind, one *does* something (perhaps only to move the body or handle an object), and then one notes the difference between what actually happens and what is inferred from previous knowledge. From this difference, one is led to a new perception or a new idea that accounts for the difference. And this process can go on indefinitely without beginning or end, in any field whatsoever.

One thing that prevents us from thus giving primary emphasis to the perception of what is new and different is that we are afraid to make *mistakes*. From early childhood, one is taught to maintain the image of "self" or "ego" as essentially perfect. Each mistake seems to reveal that one is an inferior sort of being, who will therefore, in some way, not be fully accepted by others. This is very unfortunate, for, as has been seen, all learning involves trying something and seeing what happens. If one will not try anything until he is assured that he will not make a mistake in whatever he does, he will never be able to learn anything new at all. And this is more or less the state in which most people are. Such a fear of making a mistake is added to one's habits of mechanical perception in terms of preconceived ideas and learning only for specific utilitarian purposes. All of these combine to make a person who cannot perceive what is new and who is therefore mediocre rather than original.

Evidently, then, the ability to learn something new is based on the general state of mind of a human being. It does not depend on special talents, nor does it operate only in special fields, such as science, art, music or architecture. But when it does operate, there is an undivided and total interest in what one is doing. Recall, for example, the kind of interest that a young child shows when he is learning to walk. If you watch him, you will see that he is putting his whole being into it. Only this kind of whole-hearted interest will give the mind the energy needed to see what is new and different, especially when the latter seems to threaten what is familiar, precious, secure, or otherwise dear to us.

It is clear that all the great scientists and artists had such a feeling for their work. But no matter what his occupation may be, anyone can, in principle, approach life in this way. Here, I am reminded of Anne Sullivan, who was the teacher of Helen Keller. When she came to teach this child, who was blind and deaf from an early age (and therefore unable to speak as well), she knew that she would have to treat her with complete love. However, on first seeing her "pupil," she met a "wild animal," who apparently could not be approached in any way at all. If she had seen only according to her preconceptions she would have given up immediately. But she worked with the child as best she could, with all the energies at her disposal, remaining extremely sensitively observant, "feeling out" the unknown mind of the child, and eventually *learning* how to communicate with her.

The key step here was to teach the child to form a *concept* (which she had never learned, because she had not been able to communicate with other people to any significant extent). This was done by causing her to come in contact with water in a wide variety of different forms and contexts, each time scratching the word "water" on the palm of her hand. For a long time, the child did not grasp what it was all about. But suddenly she realized that all these different experiences referred to one substance in its many aspects, which was symbolized by the word "water" scratched in her palm. This initiated a fantastic revolution in the whole of her mind, the depth and scope of which we find hard to appreciate without having experienced directly what it means to live without conceptual abstractions. As a result, where there had been a child without the ability to communicate or even to think, there was now a more or less normal human being. Thus, the discoveries of Anne Sullivan were extraordinarily creative, in helping transform the life not only of Helen Keller, but later, also of a large number of other people in similar situations.

This example is especially worth considering, because it shows by contrast how unperceptive and uncreative most parents and teachers are. Very few indeed have the love for children which makes them observant and sensitive to the *actual fact* of how children are in reality *different* from what people expect them to be, and of how an understanding of this difference might well be the key to a transformation as remarkable as that initiated by Anne Sullivan in Helen Keller.

Such an opportunity arises in many fields which may at first show little promise, especially because (at least at first) society is not in the habit of *recognizing* them to be potentially creative. Indeed, real originality and creativity imply that one does not work *only* in fields that are recognized in this way, but that one is ready in each case to inquire for oneself as to whether there is or is not a fundamentally significant difference between the actual fact and one's preconceived notions that opens up the possibility for creative and original work.

Having seen that creativity of some kind may be possible in almost any conceivable field, and that it is always founded on the sensitive perception of what is new and different from what is inferred from previous knowledge, we shall now go on to inquire in more detail into what it actually is. In other words, what does a person do when he is being original or creative that distinguishes him from one who is only mediocre?

We can begin to see the meaning of the question by asking first: "What is characteristic of the *results* of creative action, i.e. the scientific theory, the work of art, the building, the child who has been rightly brought up and educated, and so forth?" Here, we must distinguish between an occasional act of penetrating insight and the discovery of something new that is really creative. In the latter, I suggest that there is a perception of a *new basic order* that is potentially significant in a broad and rich field. This new order leads eventually to the creation of new structures having the qualities of harmony and totality, and therefore the feeling of beauty.

To understand what this means, however, we must first go into what is signified by the terms "order," "structure," "harmony," and "totality." Let us begin with order. Now, it is commonly believed that terms like "order" and "disorder" refer only to subjective judgements, which are completely dependent on the particular tastes, prejudices and opinions of different people. I wish to suggest here that order is not a purely subjective quality and that, on the contrary, judgements concerning it can have just as objective a basis as those concerning, for example, distance, time, mass, or anything else of this nature. For, as I shall try to explain presently in more detail, such judgements are based on the perceptual discrimination of *similar differences* and *different similarities*, which can be defined and communicated just as well as can be done with other qualities that are commonly recognized to be capable of an objective description.

Consider, for example, a geometrical curve, which is, in a certain way, evidently an *ordered* set of points. To express this order in a precisely communicable and perceptually testable way, we can regard the curve approximately as a set of lines of equal length. The lines are thus *similar* in their lengths, but generally *different* in their orientations. But the existence of a regular curve (rather than an arbitrary array of points) evidently depends on the *similarity of the differences*. These are, of course, immediately noted by the eye, even though our common language is generally too crude and impoverished to allow us to communicate exactly what it is that the eye has seen.

It is just because people find that they cannot communicate their very often genuine perceptions regarding the quality of order that they are inclined to assume that these perceptions are purely private and subjective. Clearly, it is necessary to avoid such a tendency to fall into confusion, by developing a language that can describe the quality of order properly. As a first step toward doing this, let us begin by considering a few simple examples of orders and curves.

Now, the simplest curve is a straight line. Here the successive segments differ only in position, and are similar in direction. Then comes the circle; successive segments also differ in direction. But the angles between them are the same, so that the differences are similar. However, the *similarities* defining the circle are *different* from those defining the straight line. This, in fact, is the essential *difference* between the two curves. The next curve is a spiral. This is obtained when successive pairs of segments differ in that they define different planes, so that the curve turns into a third dimension. The similarity of these differences leads to a regular spiral.

Evidently, it is possible to go on to higher-order differences, whose similarities generate a series of *ordered* curves of ever greater complexity. Here it is important to note that the "complexity" of a curve is in fact an objectively definable property of its order. Thus, a straight line is determined by its first step, so that it is a curve of first order. A circle is a curve of second order, determined by its first three steps. One can imagine curves requiring more and more steps to define them. Eventually, one would come to curves requiring an unlimited number of steps, which would be called "curves of infinite order." The extremely complicated paths traced by atomic particles in "chaotic" movement in a gas, or by small smoke particles in Brownian motion, would be examples of curves of infinite order.

Now, it is commonly stated that particles of the kind described above are moving in a state called "disorder." In my view, there is no such thing as "disorder," if this term is meant to indicate a *total absence of order of any kind whatsoever*. For whenever anything happens it evidently occurs in some kind of order, which can in principle be described in suitable terms. Thus, the order of planetary motion is evidently a simple one that is determined in effect by the first step (and by the forces experienced by the planet in its motion). On the other hand, the order of Brownian motion is, as has been seen, an infinite one, in the sense that it could be described only in terms of an unlimited set of similar differences. However, such a movement has certain statistical regularities or symmetries which do not depend significantly on the precise details of the path of its orbital curve. For example, in the long run and on the average the particle spends nearly the same time in any unit volume of the space that is accessible to it. And if there are many such particles, they are almost always distributed nearly uniformly in the container, at any given moment. Clearly, these features of the infinite order of Brownian movement are just as factual, communicable, and testable as are the features of the order in which an object falls to the ground or a planet moves through space. None of them is only a result of purely subjective judgements as to what would constitute "order" or "disorder."

Indeed, as has been seen, what is commonly called "disorder" is merely an inappropriate name for what is actually a certain rather complex kind of order that is difficult to describe in full detail. Our real task can, therefore, never be to judge whether something is ordered or disordered, because *everything* is ordered, and because disorder in the sense of the absence of every conceivable kind of order is an impossibility. Rather, what one really has to do is *to observe and describe the kind of order that each thing actually has*. The term "disorder" thus serves no useful purpose anywhere and is in fact always a source of confusion. What is needed to remove this confusion is to use instead a language expressed in terms of similar differences, and different similarities, which enables us in principle to describe the actual order of each thing, whatever it may be (just as a language expressed in terms of units of length enables us to describe the actual distances of things from each other).

Let us now go on to discuss the meaning of the term "structure." I wish to suggest that structure is in essence a hierarchy of orders, on many levels. Consider, for example, a house. The basically similar elements are the bricks. But these *differ* in position and orientation. When these are *ordered* in a certain array of similar differences, they make a wall. But now, the wall is an element of a *higher order*. For the different walls, arranged with suitable similarities in place and orientation, make the rooms. Likewise, the rooms are ordered to make the house, the houses to make the street, the streets to make the city, and so forth.

The principle of structure as a hierarchy of orders is evidently universal. Thus, electrons and nuclear particles ordered in a certain way make the atoms. These latter are ordered in various ways to make matter at the microscopic level, whether liquid, solid, or gaseous, crystalline or non-crystalline, and so on. This principle goes on up to the planets, the stars, the galaxies, galaxies of galaxies, continuing to be valid as far as man has been able to probe with his scientific instruments. Similarly, protein molecules ordered in a certain way make the living cell. Cells ordered in a certain way make the organs. These are ordered to make the organisms, which in turn are ordered to make the society of organisms, until we cover the whole sphere of life on earth, and perhaps ultimately extending to other planets.

It seems clear from the above that the evolutionary process of nature (which includes the development of man and his intelligent perceptions) is at least potentially of an infinite order, in the sense that it is not *fully* determined by any of its partial orders. In this respect it is similar to the random curve of Brownian motion. However, it differs from Brownian motion in that it does not tend to approach a state of complete statistical regularity or symmetry. Rather, as has been seen, each order can become the basis of a new higher order, to form a continually evolving hierarchy, leading to new structures that are generally able to order those of a simpler nature (as the nervous system orders the mechanical movements of the muscle cells). Thus, it can be seen that nature is a *creative process*, in which not merely new structures, but also new *orders of structure* are always emerging (though the process takes a very long time by our standards).

The basic principle in the development of all structure (whether natural or man-made) is clearly that each kind of order has only an *approximate* and *limited* kind of symmetry. The regular array of breaks or changes in the symmetry of one order is the basis of another level of order, and so on to higher levels. The universal validity of this principle implies, of course, not merely the possibility of the unending growth of a hierarchy of harmonious orders leading to the evolution of ever more encompassing and unified totalities. It can also lead to the possibility of *conflict* and *clash* between different orders that will produce, not harmonious and unified totalities, but rather a process of destruction and decay of the partial orders.

As happens with the notion of order itself, there is a widespread belief that the distinction between conflict and harmony is a purely private and subjective kind of judgement. One can see, however, that it is not *entirely* subjective, if one notes that conflict is a movement in which the orders of the various parts do not work together in a coherent way, such that each partial order is compatible with all the others, and indeed, in many cases, even necessary for their existence.

A very elementary example of conflict or clash can be seen in an intersection of roads. Normally, the function of a traffic signal is to help keep the orders of traffic in the two roads harmoniously coordinated. When the signal is not operating properly, then the coordination is gone, and the cars will collide at the intersection, destroying both themselves and their drivers. Or to take a more subtle example, consider the function of the digestive organs, which when a person is ill will fail to follow the normal and proper order of operation needed for the health of the organism as a whole. Or else, one can think of a cancer, whose order of growth without limit is evidently such as to clash with the processes of the body. In all these cases, what we have to deal with is, of course, not disorder or the absence of order, but, rather, *well-defined order that is functionally wrong*, in the sense that it does not lead to a harmonious totality, but rather to clash and conflict of the many partial orders.

Having seen that the perception of harmony and totality need not be a purely private kind of judgement, one can now understand in a new light the fact that the really great scientists have, without exception, all seen in the structural process of nature a vast harmony of order of indescribable beauty. It seems likely that this perception was at least as valid as were those leading to precisely defined theories and formulae permitting the exact computation of some of the detailed characteristics of matter. Indeed, every great scientific theory was in reality founded on such a perception of some very general and fundamental feature of the harmony of nature's order. Such perceptions, when expressed systematically and formally, are called "laws of nature."

To express some fundamental feature of the order of natural process in terms of a universal law is, however, actually to assert what are the basic *differences* that are relevant for the whole of this process, and what are the corresponding similarities in these differences. Thus, Newton assumed that, generally speaking, the relevant differences were in the positions and velocities of material bodies at successive moments of time. In empty space the distances covered by such bodies in similar intervals of time were assumed to be similar in magnitude and direction, thus leading to motion in a straight line at a constant speed (which is, of course, the well-known law of inertia). In the presence of matter it was assumed that these successive distances and their directions were different. However, their *differences* (which define the acceleration) were assumed to be universally similar, in the sense that similar forces would always and everywhere produce similar accelerations. When expressed in precise mathematical terms, these assumptions led to Newton's laws of motion.

A part of Newton's ideas was that the fundamental differences in position were to be thought of as being in an absolute space and taking place in an absolute time. That is to say, he supposed that space and time differences were universally similar, in such a way that different observers would all agree on what was the same interval of time and the same distance in space. Einstein's really creative insight was to see that the facts available to him (which were such as to put physical theory into a considerable state of confusion) could be clearly understood if we supposed that observers going at different speeds are actually attributing the property of simultaneity and of being at the same distance to *different* sets of events. However, he also saw that observers having similar differences of velocity would have similar differences in their ways of choosing the sets of events to which the properties of simultaneity and of being at the same distance were attributed. When expressed in precise mathematical terms, this led to the well-known Lorentz-transformation laws, which were at the foundations of the mathematical theory of relativity.

So, it is clear that Einstein's basic step was to perceive a new set of essential differences, from which there arose a new relationship of similarity, and thus a *new order of space and time*. Since space and time are fundamental to all our conceptions, this new order had to have a broad and deep significance. In terms of this new order, it became natural to ask new kinds of questions in the investigation of physical phenomena, and scientists were thus led to entirely new notions concerning the general properties of matter (which included, for example, the discovery of the equivalence of mass and energy that had such a revolutionary significance).

If one reflects on this situation, however, one will understand that Newton also perceived a new basic difference, and thus creatively initiated a new order in physics. To see this, let us go back to the ancient Greeks, who regarded the key or essential difference as being between the imperfection and corruption of earthly matter and the perfection and purity of heavenly matter (and who thus generalized the moral notion of difference between imperfection and perfection as the fundamental one, relevant for the whole of existence). The complicated movements of earthly matter were taken as revealing its imperfect nature. On the other hand, heavenly matter should express the perfection of its nature by moving in a circle, which was considered to be the most perfect of geometrical figures.

If observation had disclosed that heavenly bodies do, in fact, move in perfect circles, this would have been a tremendous discovery, tending strongly to confirm the notion that a key difference in the universe is between the perfection of heavenly matter and the imperfection of earthly matter. But when observations did not disclose this, astronomers began to accommodate the differences between fact and theory by fitting the fact to a set of circles within circles as epicycles. If a few epicycles had been enough, this too would have been a significant discovery. But when the number of epicycles began to increase greatly, one should have begun to suspect that the distinction between heavenly matter and earthly matter was not a fundamental one. But for various reasons (religious, political, psychological, etc.) this notion was not seriously entertained for a long time. Instead, there arose a tendency to focus on the utilitarian aspects of the theory of epicycles (e.g. they were useful for astrological and navigational purposes).

Although it would be wrong to discount the value of such useful computations altogether, one must nevertheless be struck by the contrast between the deep, fundamental, and all-embracing questions raised by the ancient Greeks, and the subsequent emphasis on relatively narrower, petty, and limited purposes. Thus for a long time scientists lost much of their earlier impetus toward originality and creativity, and tended instead toward the attitude of wishing mainly to accumulate potentially useful knowledge within an essentially fixed framework of concepts.

As a matter of fact, before the accumulation of such knowledge could begin to realize even its potential utilitarian value, it was necessary that a new spirit should arise which questioned the assumption of a fundamental difference between heavenly and earthly matter. In the work of Galileo and Newton, it was perceived that a much more relevant set of differences is, as has already been indicated, in the successive states of movement of each particle of matter. And in Einstein's theory further fundamental differences were assumed to be in the set of times and places that are to be taken as simultaneous and equidistant. Quantum theory brought in other fundamental differences, which we have no space to go into here.

It seems clear that the creative development of science depends quite generally on the perception of the irrelevance of an already known set of fundamental differences and similarities. Psychologically speaking, this is the hardest step of all. But once it has taken place, it frees the mind to be attentive, alert, aware, and sensitive so it can discover a new order and thus create new structures of ideas and concepts.

The relationship of a creative scientist to the results of the creative work of earlier scientists is of crucial significance here. Evidently, such a scientist cannot be similar to Einstein in the quality of creativity if he merely applies what Einstein did to new problems, or even varies, extends, and develops it so that it reveals its full implications in synthetic combinations with other theories that are already known. Nor, of course, would such a scientist be creative merely by reacting against Einstein's work or by ignoring it altogether. Rather, what is called for is that he *learns* from Einstein in the sense that he not only understands what the latter did, but also perceives the differences between the insights of Einstein and those that are now developing in his own mind as he works on the subject (which will evidently be different from Einstein's, not only because he has new knowledge, experimental and theoretical, but also for countless other reasons of a nature that it is difficult or impossible to specify in detail). It is the feeling-out of such differences that will indicate the new similarities that are appropriate to his own situation. These new similarities will eventually lead to a different set of laws of nature, which should, however, contain what was correct in Einstein's laws as special limiting cases and approximations.

Thus, a creative new perception leads, as it were, to a new order in the hierarchy of our understanding of the laws of nature, which neither imitates the older orders nor denies their validity altogether. Indeed, it serves, as it were, to help to put our knowledge of the older laws into a more appropriate order, while at the same time it extends the frontiers of knowledge in quite new ways. But, generally speaking, there is no reason to expect that any given set of natural laws will have an unlimited domain of validity. Rather, when any laws are applied beyond their proper domain, it will almost certainly be found that the corresponding fundamental differences defining nature's order in this domain eventually cease to be similar. Indeed, the *differences will now be different*. This leads in turn to new similarities and thus to the perception of new orders and the creation of new structures. So, in a way, the order and structure of our knowledge of natural law are always evolving, by a principle similar in certain ways to that of the order and structure of nature: by similar differences, leading to different similarities, in an ever-growing hierarchy of orders, that formed, as it were, a living body of natural law.

It is not merely in science that perception of relevant differences is the basic step. Actually, all perception begins with the perception of such differences. This is because the nerves accommodate to a signal that remains similar to what it was, until they produce little or no response. Then a difference suddenly stands out very sharply in awareness.

Consider, for example, what happens when one drops a coin

on a highly patterned carpet. It is usually almost impossible to see it. But when one sees a glint of metal, the coin suddenly stands out, and is clearly visible. What one actually perceived was the *difference* between the previous state of the carpet and the state with the *glint* in it. This caused one to recollect *similar differences* in past experiences, when metal objects caused such glints to appear against a non-metallic background. Thus, one can now easily see the coin, because the whole pattern of differences between it and the carpet fits into an already known pattern of similar differences.

A great deal of our perception is necessarily of this character, which is relatively mechanical, in the sense that the order, pattern, and structure of what is perceived come from the record of past experiences and thinking. To be sure, this record is varied, adapted, and adjusted so as to accommodate the presently perceived fact. But basically, it is not new.

A somewhat higher level of perception occurs when one thinks of a past order and structure that are not commonly associated with the observed set of differences. For example, one may see that the differences in some observed field of phenomena are similar to those in some rather different and, at first sight, apparently unrelated field of phenomena. So one is led to apply known kinds of ideas in new contexts. One of the most famous examples of such perception is that of Archimedes, who suddenly understood that the differences in volume of different bodies was always similar to the differences in the amount of water that they displaced. That is to say, the order of volumes of objects was seen to be similar to the order of the volumes of water displaced by them. Therefore, by measuring the amount of displaced water, one could distinguish the specific gravity of different bodies, even though their shapes were too complicated to allow their volumes to be calculated directly from their geometrical properties.

Such a penetrating insight may lead to important discoveries, and to new inventions of considerable practical importance. Yet, it is not creation. For in creation one perceives a new fundamental set of similar differences that constitutes a genuinely new order (and not merely a relationship between two or more orders that are already known). This new order leads hierarchically to a wide range of new kinds of structure. Generally speaking, an isolated penetrating insight connecting up one field with another falls short of doing all this.

Perhaps the original and revolutionary nature of a genuinely creative perception can be illustrated very strikingly if one considers the experience of Helen Keller, when she suddenly perceived the nature of conceptual abstractions. In the beginning, she had merely been aware of a series of differences: the difference between her usual state of mind and the state of being exposed to various aspects of what we know to be water (but which she, of course, did not know anything about). The clue of similar structure in the different sensations scratched on her hand on each occasion led her, at a certain point, to understand that all these differences were basically similar. This understanding was not merely a result of what she had known before, nor was it even merely the perception of a new relationship in orders that she had already encountered before. It was, in fact, the first perception of an entirely new order in the mind: the order of the concept. And when these concepts were in turn ordered in a hierarchy this led to a new structure of the mind as a whole, enabling her to communicate with others and to think for herself. Thus, not only was the teacher very creative, but, in a way, the pupil underwent a transformation that was of an even higher order of creativity.

So to sum up we may say that quite generally, in a creative act of perception, one first becomes aware (generally non-verbally) of a new set of relevant differences, and one begins to feel out or otherwise to note a new set of similarities, which do not come *merely* from past knowledge, either in the same field or in a different field. This leads to a new order, which then gives rise to a hierarchy of new orders, that constitutes a set of new kinds of structure. The whole process tends to form harmonious and unified totalities, felt to be beautiful, as well as capable of moving those who understand them in a profoundly stirring way.

Evidently, creation of this kind has been fairly rare. In the whole of human history, perhaps only a few people have achieved it. Most of the rest of human action has been relatively mediocre, though it is interlaced with flashes of penetrating insight that help to raise it above the level of mere humdrum routine. The reason is that creative work requires, above all, a creative state of mind. And, generally speaking, what we learn as children, from parents, teachers, friends, and society in general, is to have a conformist, imitative, mechanical state of mind that does not present the disturbing danger of "upsetting the apple cart." And then most of those who are not satisfied with such conformity fall into the trap of *rebelling against it*, by projecting an opposing or contrary set of ideals, and trying to conform to these. But evidently such conformity is also not creative. For reasons that are hard to specify, a few people escape both these kinds of conditioning to mechanicalness in the operation of the mind. And of these few, a very small number indeed manage to escape the gigantic conflicts, internal and external, which may be initiated by the fear of upsetting the existing state of affairs, on which our security, our happiness, and even our lives often seem to depend.

What, then, is the creative state of mind, which so few have been able to be in? As indicated earlier, it is, first of all, one whose interest in what is being done is wholehearted and total, like that of a young child. With this spirit, it is always open to learning what is new, to perceiving new differences and new similarities, leading to new orders and structures, rather than always tending to impose familiar orders and structures in the field of what is seen.

This kind of action of the creative state of mind is impossible if one is limited by narrow and petty aims, such as security, furthering of personal ambition, glorification of the individual or the state, getting "kicks" and other satisfying experiences out of one's work, and so forth. Although such motives may permit occasional flashes of penetrating insight, they evidently tend to hold the mind a prisoner of its old and familiar structure of thought and perception. Indeed, merely to inquire into what is unknown must inevitably lead one into a situation in which all that is done may well constitute a threat to the successful achievement of those narrow and limited goals. A genuinely new and untried step may either fail altogether or else, even if it succeeds, lead to ideas that are not recognized until after one is dead.

Besides, such aims are not compatible with the harmony, beauty, and totality that is characteristic of real creation. Architects will understand that the petty and limited motives of those who want to have buildings constructed has led to cities that are very hard to live in, because they are so full of the clashing orders of conflicting movements of traffic and the decaying orders of slum areas, as well as because their overall design and structure are at best mediocre, and at worst positively ugly. Something similar is involved in all men's activities in science, art, education, or what have you.

This sort of thing is clearly inevitable. For when each man in each group acts in a particular and independently determined order, how can it be otherwise than that these orders will generally be in a state of clash and conflict? (Recall, for example, the clash of traffic at an intersection without a signal, or the destruction of an organism in which is growing a cancer, whose cells multiply without regard for the order of the organism as a whole.) A similar order of chaotic clash and conflict is manifest not only in our daily lives and in our general social organization, but also in the relationships between nations, which are now such as to threaten all with annihilation.

Evidently, then, the mechanical and uncreative character of most human activity tends, at the very least, to lead to what may be called a "general mess." Perhaps in the past it may have seemed reasonable to many to hope that the net result of these myriad conflicting mechanical orders would lead in the long run to overall progress, with ever greater harmony and happiness. But more recently the actual course of the development of society has been such as to make it very difficult to believe that anything but ultimate destruction, physical and mental, is likely to emerge from the process if it goes on indefinitely.

This "general mess" is, however, not really an entirely new thing. The fact is that for a long time many people have realized that the order of society is not a genuinely healthy one. Indeed, throughout the course of history various individuals have, from time to time, tried to initiate a new and better order by means of the violent imposition of certain preconceived ideas as to what would produce a creative state of social harmony. But events have generally proved that this never works as anticipated. The reason is that a preconceived idea of producing social harmony is in reality just as mechanical and arbitrary as is the chaotic state of conflicting orders which it aims to eliminate. This is indeed the basic defect of every form of violence—that it is necessarily and inevitably mechanical. For this reason, violence can only serve to replace earlier forms of clash and conflict by others that are in many cases even more dangerous and destructive than those that were present to begin with. The desire for power to enable one violently to impose his ideas on society is therefore based on a meaningless delusion.

What is really needed to create a genuinely new order in any field whatsoever (and not merely a mechanical continuation in modified form of the conflict of fragmentary orders) is the state of mind that is continually and unceasingly observant of the fact of the actual order of the medium in which one is working. Otherwise, one's efforts are foredoomed to failure, because the order of what is done will not correspond to the actual nature of things. And this will make conflict of *some* kind inevitable. Indeed, no really creative transformation can possibly be effected by human beings, either in nature or in society, unless they are in the creative state of mind that is generally sensitive to the differences that always exist between the observed fact and *any* preconceived ideas, however noble, beautiful, and magnificent they may seem to be.

We have seen that society is in a mess, which is the result of the conflict of arbitrary and fragmentary mechanical orders of relatively independently determined actions. Any effort to *impose* an overall order in this "mess" will serve only to make it worse. What, then, is to be done? I would first suggest that it is a wrong order of approach to try first to solve the social problem. Rather, the key is in the state of mind of the individual. For as long as the individual cannot learn from what he does and sees, whenever such learning requires that he go outside the framework of his basic preconceptions, then his action will ultimately be directed by some idea that does not correspond to the fact as it is. Such action is worse than useless, and evidently cannot possibly give rise to a genuine solution of the problems of the individual and of society.

So, fundamentally, the wrong order of human action that is responsible for our basic difficulties is due to the fact that we tend to be mechanical when what is called for is creativity. Of course, there is a right place for mechanical orders of action. Thus, we must have a great many agreed conventions (such as driving on the same side of the road) which are essentially mechanical. Moreover, our machines must evidently function in a well-defined order, or else they will break down. But when we try to apply a mechanical order to the functioning of the mind as a whole, then we are extending this order beyond its proper domain. For example, when parents are not content to tell a child how to *behave* (which is in general a reasonable thing to do), but tell him what sort of person he *should be* (for example, the exhortation "Be a good boy!"), then this implies the effort to impose a mechanical pattern very deeply in the whole order in which the mind operates. A similar effort is implied when the child is told *what he should think* (on the basis of authority, to adopt certain opinions as to what is "right and proper") and *what he should feel* (love for his parents and hatred for the enemies of his country). Because the mind is not a mechanical thing, it cannot actually hold to such an order. Thus, the child who learns to be mechanically obedient cannot help harboring feelings of aggression against those whom he is supposed always to love, while the child who learns to be mechanically aggressive and dominant cannot help feeling lonely and frightened when those whom he tries to dominate fail to love him.

If we recall the notions of order discussed earlier, we could perhaps say that, like the processes of nature, those of the mind are basically of an infinite order that is always tending to evolve toward new orders, and thus to develop hierarchies constituting new kinds of structure. On the other hand, every mechanical order is limited in certain ways so that it cannot respond adequately to what is new and creative. Thus, any effort to impose a mechanical order on the mind will lead, not to the expected result, but rather to additional unforeseen reactions that *conflict with the order that one wishes to impose*. Mechanical ideas must, therefore, be restricted in their application to limited domains which can correctly be abstracted in some degree of approximation as mechanical. But, more generally, whether one is dealing with the mind or with external nature in the broader aspects, one needs to be ready at any moment to learn something that may be basically new. And this is possible only when the mind is original and creative rather than mediocre and mechanical.

If one is at all sensitive and observant, he can actually perceive just how the mind goes into a wrong order of operation when it tries to follow a mechanically imposed pattern that involves the deeper things, such as what sort of a person one is, what one should think and feel, and so on. Evidently, the mind is then in a state of contradiction, because one part of it thinks one *should not* do so. The fact is that both parts constitute mechanical and fragmentary orders of operation that conflict with each other, in the sense that they cannot be carried out together. One can actually perceive this order of conflict, which is sensed as a painful state in which one has strong wishes and urges that pull him in two directions at once.

What is called for in such a conflict is that the mind shall be able to see the irrelevance of all mechanical patterns as to what one should be, or think, or feel. Indeed, the disharmony that inevitably arises from trying to impose or follow such a pattern can come to an end only through the creative response of the mind, from moment to moment, which alone can give rise to a harmoniously ordered totality in the psyche, rather than to a structure of conflicting fragments. But because the conflict is generally very painful, the mind tends to try to escape awareness of what is happening before it has the opportunity to respond in this way. This it does by initiating a state of *confusion*.

Of course, there is a kind of *simple confusion* that tends to arise whenever we are presented with a complex array of new facts and perceptions. Normally, it takes some time to allow all this to be "sorted out." During this time, it is properly one's whole-hearted intention to arrive at a clear perception of what has previously been "mixed up." However, when the mind is trying to escape the awareness of conflict, there is a very different kind of *self-sustaining confusion*, in which one's deep intention is really to avoid perceiving the fact, rather than to sort it out and make it clear.

Whenever this is happening, we tend to say that the mind is in a state of "disorder." But in fact the mind can then be seen to be following a well-defined order that is functionally wrong (as, for example, is the order in which the digestive organs allow food to ferment, rather than to be assimilated into the blood in a proper form). The essence of this wrong order is that every time the mind tries to focus on its contradictions, it "jumps" to something else. It simply won't stay with the point. Either it continues to dart from one thing to another, or it reacts with violent excitement that limits all attention to some triviality, or it becomes dead, dull, or anesthetized, or it projects fantasies that cover up all the contradictions, or it does something else that makes one momentarily unaware of the painful state of conflict in which the mind is. This order of self-sustaining confusion tends to spread to other fields, so that eventually the whole of the mind begins to deteriorate.

When the process of general deterioration in the order of operation of the mind reaches a certain point, a person's conflicts are then said to have made him neurotic. Everybody can then recognize that there is something deeply wrong in the way such a person's mind works. However, closer observation shows that a basically similar state of conflict, covered up by self-sustaining confusion, prevails in what is commonly called the "normal" state of mind. It is this conflict and confusion in the minds of each of us that has created the "mess" in which the individual and society now find themselves. In other words, the "mess without" is *mainly* a result of the "mess within" (though of course there is a secondary action in which external conflicts also stir up internal conflicts).

So it is futile for people whose minds are in the confused state of evading awareness of the clash of conflicting orders within to hope to create either a harmonious life for the individual, or a harmonious order of society as a whole. Unless the mind first comes to a state of relatively undivided wholeness in which it is not trying to avoid awareness of unpleasant conflicts of a fundamental nature, the problems of the individual and of society cannot do other than develop according to the clash of opposing forces that are set off by our confused mechanical reactions. Indeed, it can safely be said that in the long run no really subtle, deep, and far-reaching problems can be solved in any field whatsoever, except by people who are able to respond in an original and creative way to the ever changing and developing nature of the overall fact by which they are confronted.

We have thus come to the point of seeing that the question of being clearly aware of the difference between the creative and the mechanical character of human responses goes far beyond limited fields such as art, science, and so forth. Rather, it involves the entire human race as a whole. What is needed is a generally creative quality of living in all areas of human activity. But how are we to achieve this? Given that we have generally been conditioned to mediocrity and mechanicalness, how are we to break out of this conditioning?

It seems that, in some way, each person has to *discover* what it means to be original and creative. After all, generally speaking, the childlike quality of fresh, wholehearted interest is not entirely dead in any of us. It comes in a small burst, and then it gets lost in confusion as all the old special interests, fears, desires, aims, securities, pleasures, and pains come up from the past. These twist the fresh clarity of the mind in a mechanical way, so that the capacity for originality and creation are deadened and gradually "go to sleep." As a result, the more subtle capacity for original and creative perception has by now atrophied, so that it is generally rather weak and inactive.

In this connection, I am reminded here of what happened when I first got on a horse many years ago. The man from whom it was being hired told me, "You must think faster than the horse, or else you will go where the horse wants to go." This made a deep impression on me, because it contained an important truth: that a given process can be ordered only by the intervention of a faster, finer, more subtle order of process. Thus, the rider is able, by tiny pulls on the reins, to change the overall order of movement of the horse. Likewise, the original and creative action of the mind could probably direct the mechanical function in a corresponding way. For it could see where the mechanism was going long before the latter began to gain an overwhelming momentum in that direction.

But now imagine that the mechanical jogging of the horse has put the rider to sleep. Occasionally, the rider wakes up and is horrified to see where the horse is taking him. So he corrects the direction of the horse, and the jogging soon sends him back to sleep again. Perhaps eventually the horse also begins to worry about whether he will ever be able to find his way back to the stable. So it occurs to him that he should wake up the rider. But he wants first to be sure that the rider will take him back to the stable, where he will get a good meal and a comfortable place to rest. Since his thinking is no match for the rider, he hesitates to awaken the latter, who may well direct him to an entirely different goal.

Similarly, the mechanical reactions of the mind eventually lead to the thought, "I need a creative response to get me out of this mess." But then there is the further mechanical thought, "If I get an original idea, I may make a mistake. People will condemn me. I could lose my comfortable and safe job," or whatever the case may be. So eventually the mechanical reactions are never able to be really serious in the intervention to awaken the creative action of the mind.

Is it possible in any way for creative action of the mind to awaken? In my view, this can be brought about only by the creative response of the mind itself, on those occasions in which it may happen to begin to wake up. It is as if the rider, when he was momentarily jolted out of his comfortable state of somnolence, began to be aware of the mechanical responses that were putting him back to sleep again. Perhaps in this way he could really wake up. Likewise, if one is serious about being original and creative, it is necessary for him first to be original and creative about reactions that are making him mediocre and mechanical. Then eventually the natural creative action of the mind may fully awaken, so that it will start to operate in a basically new order that is no longer determined mainly by the mechanical aspects of thought.

In thus emphasizing the need for each individual to realize the creative potentialities of the human mind, I do not wish to suggest that this is merely what I (or other people) happen to want, or what I think would be useful to society or to the individual himself. Rather, it seems to me that just as the health of the body demands that we breathe properly, so, whether we like it or not, the health of the mind requires that we be creative. That is to say, the mind is not the sort of thing that can properly act mechanically. And this is why we always fail whenever we try to be mechanical. The ultimate result is always a painful and unpleasant state of dissatisfaction and conflict, covered up by self-sustaining confusion, in which the mind "jumps" continually between incompatible orders of operation. This state not only is not creative, but actually falls far short even of the limited kind of order that is displayed by a good machine.

But, of course, to awaken the creative state of mind is not at all easy. On the contrary, it is one of the most difficult things that could possibly be attempted. Nevertheless, for the reasons that I have given, I feel that it is for each of us individually and for society as a whole the most important thing to be done in the circumstances in which humanity now finds itself. And the key is, as I have indicated, to be continually aware of and alert to the basically mechanical reactions that are always causing us to "go to sleep" again and again.

Just what are these reactions? This is too complex a question to be gone into in detail here. But, roughly, it can be said that the root of the trouble is in the confusion between what is really creative and the mechanical continuation of the results of past conditioning. For example, each person will note that, either tacitly or explicitly, he is according extremely great importance and value to certain comforts, pleasures, stimulating sources of a "tingling" sense of excitement and euphoria, secure and satisfying routines of life, actions that are necessary to his feeling of being an accepted and worthwhile sort of person, and various other mental responses that are felt to be of a *supreme degree of psychological significance*. Indeed, such responses often seem so basic to the psyche that one feels that he cannot bear to have them seriously disturbed. Even more, it may often appear that they are inseparable parts of one's "very self," so that all the creative possibilities of the mind would depend on first seeing to it that they are in a right order (as all one's physical actions depend on obtaining an adequate supply of the right kind of food). However, closer observation shows that the continuation of these responses is not really necessary for happiness and creation, and that, on the contrary, they are actually nothing but mechanical results of past conditioning, being in fact the principal barriers to real joy and creativity.

Now, as one can discover if he observes himself and other people carefully for a while, the fact is that the mind cannot help but assign supreme value in this way to whatever *appears* to be creative or necessary for creation. It is therefore clear that the confusion of the creative with the mechanical will have extremely deep and far-reaching consequences for the whole of the mind, with effects going immensely beyond more narrow and restricted kinds of conflicts. Indeed, what happens is that when the mechanical, mistaken for the creative, begins to display its inherent contradictions (so that its very existence seems to be threatened), the whole energies of mind and body are mobilized to "protect" the apparently supremely precious thoughts and feelings that are thus "endangered." As has been indicated, it is able to do this by falling into a state of self-sustaining confusion, in which it is no longer aware of its contradictory thoughts and the painful conflicts that result from them. In doing this, it lacks clear perception in almost any area that may be at all subtle. Thus, it can no longer see what is creative and what is mechanical. Indeed, the mind then starts to suppress real originality and creation, because these seem to threaten the apparently creative, but actually mechanical, center that appears to be at the heart of one's "very self." It is just this action that constitutes the process of "falling asleep."

The tendency to "fall asleep" is sustained by an enormous number of habitually applied preconceptions and prejudices, most of which are absorbed at a very early age, in a tacit rather than explicit form. Therefore, whoever is really interested in what it really means to be original and creative will have, above all, to pay careful and continual attention to how these are always tending to condition his thoughts, feelings, and overall behavior. After a while, such a person will begin to notice that almost all that is done by the individual and by society is in fact rather strictly limited by such largely tacit and essentially mechanical constraints. But as he becomes sensitively aware of how the whole process works, in himself and in others, he is likely to discover that the mind is beginning to come to a more natural state of freedom, in which all this conditioning is seen to be the triviality that it really is.

Thus, originality and creativity begin to emerge, not as something that is the result of an effort to achieve a planned and formulated goal, but rather as a by-product of a mind that is coming to a more nearly normal order of operation. And this is the only way in which originality and creativity can possibly arise, since any effort to reach them through some planned series of actions or exercises is a denial of the very nature of what one hopes to achieve. For this reason, originality and creativity can develop only if they are the essential force behind the very first step.

This means that it is up to each person to make the first step for himself, without following another, or setting up another as his authority for the definition of what creativity is and for advice on how it is to be obtained. Unless one starts to discover this for himself, rather than to try to achieve the apparent security of a well-laid-out pattern of action, he will just be deluding himself and thus wasting his efforts. To realize this fact is very difficult indeed. Nevertheless, one has to see that, to determine the order in which one functions psychologically by following some kind of pattern, is the very essence of what it means to be mediocre and mechanical.

But, after all, for thousands of years people have been led to believe that anything and everything can be obtained if only one has the right techniques and methods. What is needed is to be aware of the ease with which the mind slips comfortably back into this age-old pattern. Certain kinds of things can be achieved by techniques and formulae, but originality and creativity are not among these. The act of seeing this deeply (and not merely verbally or intellectually) is also the act in which originality and creativity can be born.

# 2

# ON THE RELATIONSHIPS OF SCIENCE AND ART

In order properly to understand the relationship between science and art, it is necessary to go into certain deeper questions which have to do with what underlies both these forms of human activity. The best point of departure for studying these questions is perhaps a consideration of the fact that man has a fundamental need to *assimilate* all his experience, both of the external environment and of his internal psychological process. Failing to do so is like not properly digesting food, thus leading to the ingestion directly into the blood of foreign proteins (such as viruses) with destructive effects, resulting from their failure to work together with the body-proteins to form a harmonious overall structural process. Similarly, psychological experiences that are not properly "digested" can work in the mind as viruses do in the body, to produce a "snow-balling" state of ever-growing disharmony and conflict, which tends to destroy the mind as effectively as unassimilated proteins can destroy the body.

Whether one is discussing food, man's natural and social environment, or ideas and feelings, the question of assimilation is always one of establishing a harmoniously ordered totality of *structural relationships*. Ever since the earliest days, man seems to have been in some ways aware of the need to do this. In primitive times, science, art, and religion, interwoven to form an inseparable whole, seem to have been the major means by which this assimilation process worked.

Science was concerned not only with practical problems of assimilating nature to man's physical needs, but also with the psychological need to *understand* the universe—to assimilate it mentally so that man could feel "at home" in it. Early creation myths, which were as much scientific in their aims as religious, certainly had this function.

As for art, it evidently helped man to assimilate the immediately perceptual aspects of experience into a total structure of harmony and beauty. It is clear that *the way* a human being perceives with his senses helps, in large measure, to make him what he is, psychologically speaking. The artist not only had to observe nature with a certain kind of objectivity that could be called the germ of a "scientific" attitude (for instance, in order to get the kind of images and ornamental patterns that he wanted), but he also very probably had an unusual sensitivity to the beauty in nature's forms and structures. By expressing this perception in the form of artistically created objects, he also helped other people to see in a more sensitive way. In addition, his work ultimately led to architecture, as well as to decorative art, which helped man to create around him a physical environment that he could assimilate into a relatively harmonious structure of perception and feeling.

Although our main interest here is the relationship between art and science, I do not think that it is possible to understand this properly without paying at least some attention to religion. Religion has been concerned centrally with the question of experiencing *all* life, *all* relationships, as one unbroken totality, not fragmented, but whole and undivided. As an excellent illustration of this fundamental aspect of religion, I am reminded of an ancient Hebrew prayer that I learned as a child, which ended with the injunction of "love God with all your heart, all your spirit, and all your might." I took this to indicate that this was really the way one is meant to *live*. One sees in this example (as in many others that will come to the mind of the reader) that a key function of religion was to teach a kind of self-knowledge, aimed at helping man to be whole and harmonious in every phase of life. To this end it was necessary, of course, to cease to be concerned excessively with narrow interests, of self, family, tribe, nation, which latter tend to break the psyche of man into conflicting fragments, making a wholehearted *total* approach to life impossible.

Of course, man's efforts at harmonious assimilation were misunderstood by many and became confused, thus leading to destructive results. Science, for example, extended the possibilities of war, plunder, and enslavement with its attendant miseries, far beyond what primitive man could do. Religion became a means of supporting the established order of society against the natural tendency for such an order to change with time. Such support was founded on speculations concerning a supposedly eternal supernatural order, which also came to give comfort and reassurance to people on the basis of illusory notions. But these functions are destructive, because *any* idea held solely in order to give pleasant feelings or to assure the stability of a particular custom or organization must ultimately lead people to think in terms of comforting and apparently satisfying illusions, rather than in terms of what is true. In this connection, art was often interwoven with religion, with the purpose of backing up the illusory aspects of religion by giving these aspects a false air of reality and concreteness, in the form of beautifully and skillfully made images and symbols of gods and supernatural forces. Similarly, scientific ideas were restricted and distorted so as not to disturb the prevailing religious mythology.

In view of the destructive effect of illusions of the kind described above, it may be said that the most significant implication of science is less in its many positive achievements than in the fact that it teaches us to look at facts in an unbiased way, *whether we like it or not*, and that it is meaningless to do otherwise. Indeed, one of the main points that I wish to make in this essay is that such a *scientific spirit* is necessary, not only in what is commonly called "scientific research," but also in art and in every phase of life, and that without this spirit, human actions are continually in danger of deteriorating into a mere response to illusion, leading to conflict and destruction.

In modern times the functions of science, art, and religion have become fragmented and confused. Science developed at an unparalleled pace in technical directions, but it seems to have parted almost completely from its role of aiding man to assimilate the universe psychologically, so that he could feel at home in a world that he understands and to the beauty of which he can respond inwardly and wholeheartedly. On the other hand, it seems that artists are not generally very seriously concerned with the scientific interest in seeing the fact, *whether one likes it or not*. Indeed, it seems that many artists (though, of course, not all) have rather widely tended to accept the current view, which regards human relationships, expressed in culture (including art, literature, music, drama, and so forth), as a field that can be manipulated at will in order to give pleasure, excitement, entertainment, and satisfaction, quite apart from questions of fact, logic, and coherence that are of central importance to the scientist.

As for religion, its function has grown more confused still.

Science has made it impossible for most people to accept the religious mythology literally. What is left is a vague and confused notion of some kind of God, along with various fragments of self-knowledge in the form of moral precepts.

Science and art have tried to take up some of the functions of religion, but so far in a rather confused way. Thus, the science of psychology aims at a kind of self-knowledge, leading a person to try to make a "useful" and a "profitable" adjustment to society. But man's essential illness today is his feeling of fragmentation of existence, leading to a sense of being alien to a society that he has himself created, but does not understand. Thus, he cannot assimilate his whole field of experience into a totality felt to be beautiful, harmonious, and meaningful, with the result that a mere "adjustment" to the current state of affairs is not felt by most people to be really adequate.

Art has also entered the field of self-knowledge. Many artists have tried in their work to express the present state of confusion, uncertainty and conflict, probably hoping that if these are given a visible shape and form, then somehow one can obtain mastery over them. This is a resurgence of a primitive "magical" way of thinking, a way that may have been the best that primitive man could do, but that is surely inadequate today, even if it was perhaps somewhat useful in earlier times. The fact is that no conflict is ever resolved merely by expressing it in visible or audible form. One may perhaps feel better for a while in doing this, but actually the conflict generally goes on as before, the better feeling being largely based on illusion. As was clear in the best teachings of ancient religions, the proper way to deal with conflict is to look at it directly by being aware of the full meaning of what one is doing and thinking.

Science can now help us to understand ourselves in this way by giving factual information about brain structure and function, and how the mind works. Then there is an art of self-knowledge, which each person has to develop for himself. This art must lead one to be sensitive to how his basically false approach to life is always tending to generate conflict and confusion. The role of art here is therefore not to provide a symbolism, but rather to teach the *artistic spirit* of sensitive perception of the individual and particular phenomena of one's own psyche. This spirit is needed if one is to understand the relevance of general scientific knowledge to his own special problems, as well as to give effect to the scientific spirit of seeing the fact about one's self as it is, *whether one likes it or not*, and thus helping to end conflict.

Such an approach is not possible, however, unless one also has the spirit that meets life wholly and totally. We still need this *religious spirit*, but today we no longer need the religious mythology, which is now introducing an irrelevant and confusing element into the whole question.

It would seem, then, that in some ways the modern person must manage to create a total approach to life which accomplishes what was done in earlier days by science, art, and religion, but in a new way that is appropriate to modern conditions of life. An important part of such an action is to see what the relationship between science and art *now actually is*, and to understand the direction in which this relationship might develop.

One of the basic reasons for the present tendency of science and art to remain separate and apparently not closely related is the current scientific view of the universe. In earlier times man believed that he had a central role in the universe, which helped give meaning to his life. With the Copernican revolution, the earth came to be regarded as a grain of dust in an immense, meaningless, mechanical universe, while man was seen as less than a microbe on this grain of dust. Surely, this view has had a very great psychological impact on mankind quite generally. But is it true that science *necessarily* implies a completely meaningless and mechanical character to the universe?

Some light is thrown on this question by considering the fact that most scientists (and especially the most creative ones, such as Einstein, Poincaré, Dirac, and others like them) feel very strongly that the laws of the universe, as disclosed thus far by science, have a very striking and significant kind of *beauty*, which suggests that deeply they do not really look at the universe as a mere mechanism. Here, then, is a possible link between science and art, which latter is centrally oriented towards beauty.

Now, there is a common notion that beauty is nothing more than a subjective response of man, based on the pleasure that he takes in seeing what appeals to his fancy. Nevertheless, there is much evidence that beauty is not an arbitrary response that happens to "tickle" us in a pleasing way. In science, for example, one sees and feels the beauty of a theory only if the latter is ordered, coherent, harmonious with all parts generated naturally from simple principles, and with these parts working together to form a unified total structure. But these properties are necessary not only for the beauty of a theory, but also for its truth. Of course, in a narrow sense, no theory is true unless it corresponds to the facts. But as we consider broader and broader kinds of theories, approaching those of cosmology, this notion becomes inadequate. Indeed, as has recently been pointed out in a television program by Professor Hermann Bondi, who is an authority in the field, we now have two rival cosmological theories, one due to Einstein, and the other to Hoyle.[1] The unique new situation prevailing at present is that for the foreseeable future it will not be possible to make experimental tests that could discriminate between these theories on a factual basis. We shall then have to decide between them, first, on the basis of *beauty* and, second, on the basis of which one of them helps us better to understand the general facts of science, to *assimilate* such scientific experience into a coherent totality.

To throw light on this newly developing kind of situation in science, one may note that the word "true" has a spectrum of meanings, lying between two limiting cases. First, as has already been indicated, a "true" idea corresponds to the facts. But then, "true" also means "true to self," as when we talk about a "true line" or a "true man." In the broad sense with which cosmology is concerned, the universe as a whole is to be understood as "true to itself"—a unified totality developing coherently in accordance with its basic principles. And as man appreciates this, he senses that his own response with feelings of harmony, beauty, and totality is parallel to what he discovers in the universe. So, in a very important way, the universe is seen to be less alien to man than earlier excessively mechanistic points of view seemed to indicate.

Here, it seems, is a key link between art and science. For to the scientist, both the universe and his theory of it are beautiful, in much the same sense that a work of art can be regarded as beautiful—in effect, that it is a coherent totality, in the way described above. Of course, the scientist and the artist differ in a very important respect. For the scientist works mainly at the level of very abstract ideas, while his perceptual contact with the world is largely mediated by instruments. On the other hand, the artist works mainly on creating concrete objects that are directly perceptible without instruments. Yet, as one approaches the broadest possible field of science, one discovers closely related criteria of "truth" and "beauty." For what the artist creates must be "true to itself," just as the broad scientific theory must be "true to itself." Thus, neither scientist nor artist is really satisfied to regard beauty as that which "tickles one's fancy." Rather, in both fields structures are somehow evaluated, consciously or unconsciously, by whether they are "true to themselves," and are accepted or rejected on this basis, *whether one likes it or not*. So the artist really needs a scientific attitude to his work, as the scientist must have an artistic attitude to his.

It seems to me that in the question of truth and beauty one finds what is really the deepest root of the relationship between science and art. On the basis of this understanding we can now study the relationship of science and art more broadly.

In early days both science and art tended to work largely in terms of images, representations, symbols, and so on. Thus in science it was commonly thought that theories and instrumental observations were simple reflections of the world as it is. Later, it became evident that such a simple reflection process cannot give the whole story. Each theory and each instrument selects certain aspects of a world that is infinite, both qualitatively and quantitatively, in its totality. According to modern physics (especially the quantum theory), when one comes down to the atomic and subatomic level of size, the observing instrument is even *in principle* inseparable from what is to be observed, so that this instrument cannot do other than "disturb" the observed system in an irreducible way: and indeed it even helps to create and to give form to what is observed. One may compare this situation to a psychological observation, which can likewise "disturb" the people being studied, and thus take part in the process that one wants to learn about, as well as "create" and shape some of the very phenomena that can be observed.

There has been in physics a gradually increasing awareness that scientific theories cannot be mere reflections of nature. Rather, as has recently been suggested by Kuhn,[2] they are more like "paradigms," in effect, simplified but typical examples, the study of which illuminates nature as a whole for us, by revealing the essential relationships that are significant for observation and experiment. In a similar way, the physicist's instruments enter into a "paradigm relationship" with natural processes at the atomic levels, in which these processes reveal their essential order and structure in a simplified but "typical" way. Once we understand the paradigm relationships we can look afresh at nature in all its complexity, and see it in a new light in a wide range of more particular and limited kinds of questions.

Now it should be evident that artists also make what may be called "paradigm" structures. No good picture is exactly or even mainly a *mere* reflection of its subject matter. Thus, a painting by Rembrandt is not just an image or symbol of the person who appears in it, but rather, by heightening certain features and simplifying others, the artist brings out a "typical" aspect of character having a broad or even universal human relevance. So science and art have *always* been deeply related in this way because both have really been concerned mainly with the creation of paradigms, rather than with a mere reflection or description of subject matter.

The move away from imitative representation of nature in science, and toward the creation of what may be called a "pure paradigm," was anticipated by a corresponding movement in mathematics. Thus, mathematical expressions were originally regarded as *symbolizing* the properties of real things. But with the development of what is called the "axiomatic approach," mathematical expressions ceased to be regarded as *basically* symbolic of something else. Rather, they were *initially* given no meanings in themselves, all their meanings being in their relationships to other terms in a theory, these relationships having to be expressed as purely abstract *mathematical operations*. In this way they became elements of *structures of ideas*. Just as a brick in itself does not represent or symbolize anything else, but has all its "meaning" in the structures that can be made of bricks, so a mathematical term gets all its meaning by participating in mathematical structures created and developed by mathematicians and scientists.

Parallel with this new approach to mathematics, the notion of scientific theories as "paradigms" rather than as symbols, representations, or simple reflections of nature fits quite naturally. Such theories are creations of the scientist, evaluated partly on the basis of their beauty—harmony, order, "elegance," unified totality, and so forth—and partly by their ability to help us understand broad ranges of scientific fact—that is, to assimilate them into a yet broader coherent structure. Such understanding includes the ability to suggest new relationships that are worthy of further investigation, both theoretical and experimental. Thus, the theory plays a dynamic and creative role, not restricted to a mere passive understanding of what is already known, but also

going on to "keep ahead" of knowledge in certain ways, antici-
pating what may come later, as well as suggesting new
"paradigm relationships" with nature, to be established in experiment, and to serve as a basis for further theory creation on a yet
higher level.

It seems very interesting that the development away from
representation and symbolism, and toward what may be called
"pure structure" that took place in mathematics and in science,
was paralleled by a related development in art. Beginning with
Monet and Cézanne and going on to the Cubists and to
Mondrian, there is a clearly detectable growth of the realization
that art need not represent or symbolize anything else at all, but
rather that it may involve the creation of something new—"a
harmony parallel to that of nature," as Cézanne put it. It is surely
significant that this direction of evolution has been continued in
a new very active school of art which has included those who are
called by various related names, such as "constructionists" and
"structurists." Although these artists are by no means in
complete agreement as to their aims and beliefs, one can see in
their work and in what they write the implication that ultimately
the artist must start from certain basic (and generally three-
dimensional) structural elements, which have in *themselves* no
meaning, but which participate in forming a structure created by
the artist, and which in this way take on all their meaning. As
happens with scientific theories, such artistic creations can be
beautiful in themselves, and also serve as simplified paradigm
cases of structure, throwing light on the general nature of structure as perceived directly at the level of the senses (rather than as
mediated by scientific instruments). In this way, art too can play
a dynamic role, corresponding to that of science, because it is
able to lead to new ways of perceiving man's environment, and
these in turn can become the basis for further artistic creation on
a yet higher level.

It seems remarkable that science, art, and mathematics have
thus been moving in related directions, toward the development
of what is, in effect, a mode of experiencing, perceiving, and
thinking in terms of *pure structure*, and away from the *comparative, associative, symbolic* method of responding mainly in terms
of something similar that was already known earlier in the past.
Such an approach is as yet in its infancy, so that there would be
little reason, especially in a brief essay of this kind, to attempt to
evaluate the works of specific artists, scientists, or mathematicians

with regard to this trend toward taking structure to be the essence of all experience. It seems sufficient at this point to call attention to the very widespread evolution in related directions in several different fields of human endeavor.

To me, the principal significance of this direction of evolution is that it has the potentiality for indicating a new kind of response to all types of experience. That is to say, one has seen in mathematics, science, and art a set of paradigm cases in which one can respond directly to perceived structures and not merely in terms of a comparative, associative, symbolic evocation of habitual patterns of ideas, feelings, and actions that were laid down in the past. Such a possibility, presenting itself most simply in these fields, may then be realized more broadly, ultimately perhaps spreading to the whole of life. In this way, it is possible that an important contribution could be made to solving modern man's problem of creating a more harmonious and wholehearted approach to life. For a great deal of the fragmentation of existence has always derived from attachment to habitual modes of thinking, perceiving, and action which are no longer appropriate and which tend to come into conflict with the structure of the fact as it is. Anything which can teach man what it means to see this fact afresh, creatively, even in some restricted set of fields, such as the sciences, art, and mathematics, could also help in changing man's general approach to life in a corresponding way.

In view of the deep relationships between art and science that have been indicated here, what is the proper kind of connection between scientific and artistic work? It is first of all clear that there is no reason for scientist and artist simply to imitate each other, or mechanically to apply the other's results in his own field. For example, it would evidently be of little use for the scientist to begin with a particular work of art and try to translate or adapt its structure, so that it would become the basis of a scientific theory, expressing the laws and regularities of nature. For the scientist must think in terms of *abstract axiomatic concepts* and *instrumental data* which are extremely different from the basic *perceptual structure* of space, light, color, and form within which the artist works. To be sure, science and art have had a common origin in the distant past. But meanwhile, these two in reality complementary ways of coming into contact with the world have diverged and become very different. Their real unity is therefore to be apprehended only in a rather subtle way.

What the scientists can learn from art is first of all to appreciate the artistic spirit in which beauty and ugliness are, in effect, taken as sensitive emotional indicators of truth and falsity. Here, one must run counter to the popular image of the scientist as a cold, unemotional sort of fish interested only in "hard-headed" practical extensions of man's mastery over nature. If one talks with typical scientists one soon discovers that, in fact, few of them have more than a secondary and incidental interest in practical applications of their ideas. Such a discussion soon reveals that what really interests scientists most deeply is the development of an understanding leading to the assimilation of nature. Thus, many physicists are tremendously excited by the notion that *all* matter, from the most distant galaxies to the earth, including human beings, is constituted of similar atoms. In this way, they feel that somehow they are mentally assimilating the whole universe in which we live. And some of the most creative scientists (such as Einstein and Poincaré) have indicated that in their work they are often moved profoundly, in a way that the general public tends to believe happens only to artists and other people engaged in what are regarded as "humanistic" pursuits. Long before the scientist is aware of the details of a new idea, he may "feel" it stirring in him in ways that are difficult or impossible to verbalize. These feelings are like very deep and sensitive probes reaching into the unknown, while the intellect ultimately makes possible a more detailed perception of what these probes have come into contact with. Here, then, is a very fundamental relationship between science and art, which latter evidently must work in a similar way, except that the whole process culminates in a sensually perceptible work of art, rather than in an abstract theoretical insight into nature's structural process.

What can the artist learn from science? Here, it appears reasonable to me to suppose that as no particular work of art can be simply adapted or translated into a scientific or mathematical theory, so no particular theory of this kind can simply be translated or adapted to determine the structure of a work of art. Instead, I should think that what the artist could appropriately hope to learn from science is something far more subtle than this. First of all, it must seem that he could appreciate the scientific spirit of an unbiased objective approach to structure, which demands that it be internally coherent, and coherent with relevant facts, *whether one likes it or not*. Understanding that this requirement is just as relevant in art as in science, one may thus perhaps be helped to see why art is not properly to be considered as an arbitrary action intended mainly to give pleasure, satisfaction, or emotional release. Rather, just as scientific truth is found to be inseparable from artistic beauty, so artistic beauty may be seen to be inseparable from truth in the scientific sense, when the latter is given its broadest possible meaning.

To be sure, the scientist must test his truths with the aid of instrumental observations and mathematical equations, while the artist must do so with direct perception, in a more subtle way that is much harder to explain verbally. In spite of this difference, however, it seems to me that art has, and always has had, a certain factual aspect, in the sense that a good work of art must be coherent in itself, as well as with the basic natural laws of space, color, form, light, and of how they must be perceived. It does not seem to be really possible for the artist to manipulate these in a completely arbitrary way, directing his work *merely* by the criterion of producing something that is pleasing to himself and to other people (although it must be said that many artists and art critics write as if this actually was the case).

Finally, there are more specific ways in which the scientist and the artist can learn from each other about *structure*, which is really of central interest in both fields. The fact is that the deepest and most general scientific ideas about space, time, and the organization of matter have their roots largely in abstraction from perceptual experience, mainly visual and tactile. The new evolution of art can help open the viewer's eyes to seeing structure in new ways. As has already been indicated, the value of this to the scientist is not basically in the particular idea that a work of art or a statement by an artist suggests. Rather, it is in a new general understanding of structure at the perceptual level, which is relevant to every field of experiencing. From this, the scientist can form new abstract ideas of space, time, and the organization of matter.

I have personally discovered that through talking with artists and correspondence with them, as well as through seeing their work, I have been greatly helped in my scientific research. *The main effect of these contacts was to lead me to look with a fresh view at structure as I perceived it directly with the senses*. As a result, it became clear to me that current scientific and mathematical notions of structure may have only limited domains of validity. For if one looks again at the kind of perceptual contact with the world from which existing scientific and mathematical concepts have ultimately been abstracted, one sees that a great many as yet unexplored directions of abstraction have, in reality, been open all the time. In this way, the mind is freed to consider new ideas of structure, rather than to go on with comparative, associative symbolic thinking in terms of habitual patterns laid down in the past.

What has been described above may well indicate an important potential direction for the evolution of a further relationship between science and art. Vice versa, new scientific notions of structure may be significant to the artist, not so much because they suggest particular ideas to be translated into artistic form, but, rather, because if they are understood at a deep level they will change one's way of thinking about *everything*, including art.

In this connection, I have discovered in my scientific work that in the long run it is less important to learn of a particular new way of conceiving structure abstractly, than it is to understand how the consideration of such new ideas can liberate one's thought from a vast network of preconceptions absorbed largely unconsciously with education and training and from the general background. It seems to me that with regard to this question of preconceptions the situation should be basically similar in every field of creative work, whether this be scientific, artistic, or of any other nature. For by becoming aware of preconceptions that have been conditioning us unconsciously we are able to *perceive* and to *understand* the world in a fresh way. One can then "feel out" and explore what is unknown, rather than go on, as has generally been one's habit, with mere variations on old themes, leading to modifications, extensions, or other developments within the framework of what has already been known, either in one's own field, or in a closely related form in some other field. Thus, one's work can begin to be really creative, not only in the sense that it will contain genuinely original features, but also in that these will cohere with what is being continued from the past to form one harmonious, living, evolving totality.

More generally, it seems clear that everyone, whatever his field of work, could benefit from the kind of creative liberation of perception as a whole that is implied by a deep understanding of the relationship between science and art. For this would help free both the abstract intelligence and immediate sense perception from conditioning due to preconceptions and habitual responses at various levels. An understanding of this kind would, however, require a much more thorough exploration of the question of the proper relationship between science and art than has been carried out in this essay.

What is most relevant in such an exploration is to discern the basic and essential *differences* between the scientific and the artistic ways of observing and understanding structure. The harmony of these different but complementary modes in which a human being can respond to the world will surely constitute a much deeper and more significant relationship than would a mere similarity of certain concepts of structure in the two fields. And this harmony must evidently depend on questions that are more fundamental than those that can be properly treated in terms of either field alone, questions such as those involved in understanding what is really to be meant by beauty, truth, order, structure, or creation. By giving deeper insights into these, a study of the relationship of science and art can enrich both fields, as well as many other aspects of human life which also arise from these deep roots. For these roots are at the basis of humanity's process of assimilating all experience into one dynamic and creative totality, a process on which depends his physical and mental health, his joy in life, and, ultimately perhaps, the continuation of human life on this planet.

## NOTES

1   Since the first publication of this essay in 1968, the consensus of the physics community has opted for Einstein's view, commonly referred to as the "Big Bang" (Ed.).
2   Kuhn, T. (1962) *The Structure of Scientific Revolutions*. Chicago and London: University of Chicago Press.

# 3

# THE RANGE OF IMAGINATION

## On imagination and fancy

The power to imagine things that have not been actually experienced has, on the one hand, commonly been regarded as a key aspect of creative and intelligent thought. On the other hand, this power of imagination has equally commonly been regarded as a rather passive and mechanical capacity to arrange and order the images of thought arising associatively out of memory, with the aid of which the mind may at best make routine sorts of adjustments, and at worst contrive to deceive itself in such a way as may be conducive to its own pleasure, comfort, and superficial satisfaction.

As Owen Barfield has brought out so well in his book *What Coleridge Thought*,[1] such a distinction between two extreme forms of imagination was taken by Coleridge to be the nature of thought as a whole. Coleridge gave the name "primary imagination" to the one extreme and the name "fancy" to the other. "Primary imagination" is, for Coleridge, an act of creative perception through the mind, in which the images are generally fresh and original rather than derived from memory, and on which all the differences and manifold features arise naturally and harmoniously as aspects or sides of a single undivided whole. At the other extreme, "fancy" (which is actually derived from the word "fantasy") is mainly a construction involving the putting together of basically separate and distinct images already available from the memory. Coleridge meant it to include not only the routine, passive, and often self-deceptive evocation of images by association, but also a wide range of more active and intelligent modes of thinking, starting from a simple everyday arrangement first planned out in the mind, and going on to composition, design, and possibly invention, in fields such as literature, art, and science.

Between these two extremes of primary imagination and fancy is a whole range of possibilities through which Coleridge suggested that thought actually moves. He did not regard the two extremes as entirely separate and distinct. Rather, in his terms, they are the two basic poles of thought. That is to say, the energy and ordering action underlying thought as a whole arises through a kind of tension between the two poles. (As in physics, the action of electrical forces on charged particles can be looked at as arising in a field that expresses a sort of tension in the space between positive and negative charges.)

However, as Owen Barfield has brought out in some detail, Coleridge was ambiguous as to the nature of the relationship between primary imagination and fancy. The very term "primary imagination" would tend to suggest that in some sense fancy should be taken as a sort of "secondary imagination" so that the two differ mainly in being different degrees or orders of what is basically the same quality. He frequently suggests in his writings that this is indeed his point of view. On the other hand, he also implies in other parts of his writings that primary imagination and fancy differ in kind or in quality. So ultimately the meaning of this basic distinction is not clear.

## Imaginative insight and imaginative fancy in scientific research

In the present essay, I should like to go further into the implications of this question, from a point of view in which one regards imagination universally as a power to display the activity of the mind as a whole through mental images. What Coleridge considers as primary imagination will then be considered as the display through such images of creative and original *insight*, while what he regards as fancy will be taken to be the corresponding display of the more mechanical and routine aspects of thought. Thus, the one activity, indicated by the word "imagination," is to be distinguished mainly according to the order of its *content*, which moves between the extremes of imaginative insight and imaginative fancy.

It has to be kept in mind, however, that this way of looking at the subject is not meant as a definite conclusion, but rather as an inquiry or exploration into what can be learned by seeing the polarity pointed out by Coleridge in a different way. In carrying out this inquiry, I shall begin by giving some emphasis to the field of science, with which I am relatively familiar, though later I shall go on to consider the implications of this work for more general fields.

The most creative and original aspect of scientific work has generally been in the development of *theories*, especially those having such a broad and deep significance that they are felt to be universally relevant. We may obtain a significant hint or clue to what is involved here by noting that the word "theory" derives from the Greek "theoria," which has the same root as "theater," in a verb meaning "to view" or "to make a spectacle." This suggests that the theory is to be regarded primarily as a way of looking at the world through the mind, so that it is a form of insight (and not a form of knowledge of what the world is). Thus, in the field of science the extreme of imaginative insight can best be studied by giving attention to the origin and development of fundamental theories which aim at some universal sort of significance.

For example, in ancient times men had the fundamental theory that celestial matter was different in kind from earthly matter, so that it was natural for earthly objects to fall and for celestial objects, such as the moon, to remain up in the sky. With the coming of the modern era, however, scientists began to develop the point of view that there is no essential difference between earthly matter and celestial matter. This implied, of course, that heavenly objects, such as the moon, ought to fall. But for a long time men did not notice this implication. In a sudden flash of mental perception, Newton *saw* that as the apple falls, so does the moon, and so indeed do all objects. The fact that the moon never reaches the surface of the earth, while the apple does, was explained by the tangential motion possessed by the moon, but not by the apple. This tangential motion continually accelerates the moon away from the center of the earth, at a rate which balances the falling motion so that the orbit remains approximately a circle, at a very nearly constant distance from the earth.

By considering the behavior of matter more generally, Newton was led to the theory of universal gravitation, in which all objects were seen as falling toward various centers (the earth, the sun, the planets, etc.). This constituted a new way of *looking* at the heavens, in which the movements of the planets were no longer regarded in terms of the ancient notion of an essential difference between heavenly matter and earthly matter. Rather, one considered these movements in terms of different rates of fall of all matter, heavenly and earthly, toward various centers. And when something was seen not to be accounted for in this way, we often discovered new and as yet unseen planets, toward which celestial objects were falling. In this way, the new concept of universal gravitation demonstrated its fruitfulness by showing itself to be capable, not only of explaining already known facts, but also of helping direct our minds and our physical observations to hitherto unknown facts and even to hitherto unknown kinds of facts.

The movement of insight in which Newton suddenly realized that the moon *is* falling, even though it never reaches the earth, was evidently quite different from the ordinary process of discursive thought, in which one step follows another more or less logically, over a period of time. Rather, it was an extreme example of something that everybody experiences when he is thinking about a problem containing a number of contradictory or confused factors. Suddenly, in a flash of understanding, involving in essence no time at all, a new totality appears in the mind, in which this contradiction and confusion have vanished. This new totality is at first only *implicit* (i.e. unfolding) through some mental image which, as it were, contains the main features of the new perception spread out before our "mental vision." Perception involving this display, which is inseparable from the act of primary perception itself, is what may be called *imaginative insight* (or creative imagination). Such a display plays a necessary part, because with its aid the mind can apprehend the meaning of what has been created in the flash of understanding. From this apprehension, the mind can go on to think and to reason out more and more of the consequences implied by the new insight.

It is in this latter process that imaginative fancy (or constructive imagination) begins to play an important part. For example, in Newton's case it was necessary to have a relatively precise notion as to just how fast an object will fall. In developing such a notion, we may generally begin by putting forth a *hypothesis* (a supposition), which has to be tested by experiments and observations. If a given hypothesis "passes" such a test, it is accepted as a particular realization of the primary insight. If not, it is necessary to seek further hypotheses, until one is found that fits in with the available experimental facts and observations. However, even after such a hypothesis has been found to be acceptable in this way, it may be shown in later tests to be incorrect or of limited validity. It is then necessary, of course, to go on with the search for yet further hypotheses, until one is found that will fit the new facts. And so, a deep insight of universal significance, such as that of Newton, may in principle lead to an indefinite development of more and more detailed hypotheses.

In this process of development, hypotheses may often be suggested by images already available in other contexts, the relevance of which may be indicated by a detailed consideration of the available facts. Thus, from the data known to him, Newton was able to show that the moon falls considerably more slowly than an object at the surface of the earth. This meant that the force of gravitation must decrease in some way with the distance. But the question was: "Just how fast does it decrease?" It is quite possible that the precise form of the hypothesis adopted by Newton may have been suggested by calling to mind some already available image, such as that of the light intensity from a radiant object, which was already known to fall off as the inverse square of the distance. So then, the thought would arise naturally: "As with light, so perhaps with gravitation." Even if in actual fact it may not have been this image, but perhaps some other one, that suggested the inverse square law, the essential point remains that hypotheses generally involve new forms, arrangements, connections, and meanings of images already available in the mind. So, a hypothesis is primarily a form of fancy, or of constructive thought, the validity of which has to be continually tested by further appeals to observed fact.

It has to be kept in mind, however, that the distinction between insight and hypothesis is not a hard and fast one. Thus, even to notice that the rate of fall of intensity of light from an object that is a light source may be relevant to the rate of decrease of gravitational force from such an object, requires a certain imaginative insight. However, what is crucial here is that this involves the perception of a relationship between two already known sorts of images (the light intensity from an object and the force exerted by an object), while Newton's primary insight involved a fresh and original total perception displayed through a single new *kind* of image (an object that is falling, but that never reaches the earth in its fall).

On the other hand, it must also be kept in mind that even

Newton's insight was not *totally* free of known types of images, as his thought still contained certain familiar images such as those of material objects in motion through space. So the full description of what is happening here is rather more complex than we have thus far indicated. Insight and fancy are in fact never separated. They are both present in every step (even at the level of experiment and observation, a considerable degree of insight is needed to see what the fact actually means). However, in any particular case there is a different degree of emphasis in each of the two extremes. Thus, in Newton's perception of the primary notion of universal gravitation the side of insight was much more heavily emphasized than in the action involved in the proposal of the hypothesis of the inverse square law.

Insight and fancy are, in the first instance, two qualitatively different modes of operation of the mind as a whole. So, in this sense, Coleridge was right to say that they are different in kind. However, as has been pointed out above, each act of discovery always contains both sides, inseparably connected and related. Indeed, a content that was first perceived as an insight passes over into the domain of fancy, and a content first seen in the domain of fancy may be the key clue to a new insight. Through such a process of continual transition, insight and fancy come to reflect each other. But, more deeply, they interpenetrate and ultimately they are seen to be only two views of what is one undivided and whole mental movement. However, as indicated before, at any moment this movement may emphasize one side or the other. And thus Coleridge was right to say that the difference is also one of degree. But perhaps through this inquiry we may have come to a more clear view of this situation, which, in Coleridge's language, could be called "a polarity between kind and degree" (or, in Hegel's language, "the unity of quality and quantity").

A full understanding of the relationship between insight and fancy requires us to note, however, that no form of insight remains relevant and fruitful indefinitely. Thus, after several centuries of working very well, the Newtonian form of insight, when extended into new domains, eventually led to unclear results. In these new domains, new forms of insight were developed (the theory of relativity and quantum theory). These gave a radically different picture of the world from that of Newton (though the latter was, of course, found to be still valid in a limited domain). If we supposed that theories gave true knowledge, corresponding to "reality as it is," then we would have to conclude that Newtonian theory was true until around 1900, after which it suddenly became false, while relativity and quantum theory suddenly became truth. Such an absurd conclusion does not arise, however, if we say that theories are ways of looking which are neither true nor false, but rather clear and fruitful in certain domains, and unclear and unfruitful when extended beyond these domains.

This means, of course, that there is no way to prove or disprove a theory (especially if it aims at a universal sort of significance). For even if a particular realization of the theory is disproved, it is generally possible to find an alternative hypothesis allowing the theory to be maintained. Ultimately, we have to decide between such an attempt to save the old theory and the attempt to create a radically new kind of theory. This has to be done with the aid of more general judgements, such as that of whether the net result is clear, simple, beautiful, generally adequate and fruitful, and so forth. These involve a kind of aesthetic perception of harmony or disharmony within the overall structure of the theory, as well as between theory and the total body of fact available, similar to that needed in the visual arts and in music.

On the other hand, when a hypothesis is tested, the judgement of its validity is usually based on the simple fact of whether there is a *correspondence* between some of the inferences drawn from it (e.g. numerical predictions) and appropriate features of the observed fact. So we have to be careful not to confuse the testing of the hypotheses with the (basically aesthetic) judgement as to whether or not one regards it as worthwhile to go on with a given general line of theory. The ability to make this judgement properly is perhaps one of the key qualities which are required for a creative and original step, rather than a continuation or development of an insight that is already available.

The interplay of theory and hypothesis indicated in this discussion can be brought out by considering some of the lines of thinking that helped lead Einstein to the special theory of relativity.

Toward the end of the nineteenth century, there developed a great deal of confused evidence concerning the properties of light. On the one hand, from the electromagnetic theory, which had explained the then known properties of light very well, one concluded that light was a form of wave motion, consisting of oscillations of the electromagnetic field. The speed of these waves was calculated from the theory and found to be in agreement with that observed experimentally. The theory implied, however, that the speed of light, as measured relative to an observer moving in the direction of a light wave, should be less than that measured by an observer who is not moving in this way. We can see why this follows by considering a sound wave, which moves through air at a certain speed. An observer on an airplane moving in the direction of a sound wave would find that the speed of this wave relative to him was less than that relative to that of an observer fixed on the ground. Indeed, if the airplane speeds up it can catch up with the sound wave, and eventually overtake it by going faster than sound. When this happens, the observer on the airplane does not hear any of the sound produced by the airplane, because this latter is "left behind" as a shock wave.

On the other hand, actual measurements with light did not show this sort of behavior at all. Rather, they showed that all observers obtained the *same* speed of light, regardless of their speed relative to each other. These experiments implied, for example, that if a rocket ship accelerated to nine-tenths of the speed of light relative to the earth, an observer inside the ship would still obtain the same measured speed of light as would be obtained by an observer at rest on the earth. This was, of course, very puzzling. Many attempts were made by means of various *hypotheses* to explain the fact, while retaining the general lines of Newton's theory. But such explanations of a given feature led only to a paradox or puzzle in some other feature.

Einstein's thinking on this question did not center, however, on explaining the detailed experimental facts with the aid of hypotheses. Rather, like Newton, he gave his main attention to broad and deep questions relating to general concepts that had previously been largely implicit and taken for granted in a rather habitual way. Thus, at the age of fifteen he asked himself the question "What would happen if one moved at the speed of a light ray and looked in a mirror?" The light from one's face would never reach the mirror. Evidently, there is something strange about an object supposed to move at the speed of light.

From our more modern vantage point, we can bring out this strangeness even more by considering the atomic constitution of all matter. According to the generally accepted theory, the atoms that make up any object are held in a certain relatively fixed structure by the balance of the attractive and repulsive electrical forces between the charged particles (electrons and protons) out of which the atoms are in turn constituted. And according to the electromagnetic theory, when such an object reached and overtook the speed of light, each atom would leave its electromagnetic force field behind it, as a "shock wave" similar to that which arises when an airplane exceeds the speed of sound. Because there were no longer any forces holding them together, the atoms would drift apart. Any attempt to make a material object exceed the speed of light would therefore lead to its disintegration.

It seems clear that there is a fundamental difference between the theoretical significance of the speed of light and that of any other speed (such as that of sound waves). For it seems that insoluble difficulties and paradoxes arise from supposing that a material object can exceed the speed of light. Einstein already had a premonition of these difficulties, when he asked what would happen if one could move with a light ray. So, as Newton answered the question "Why doesn't the moon fall?" in a surprising way by saying that it *does* fall, so Einstein answered his own question in a correspondingly surprising way by saying, "No material object can actually reach the speed of light." In other words, the speed of light has a new quality. It is not something that can be overtaken, but rather it is more like a horizon. No matter how far we go, the horizon remains the same relative to us.

Einstein's new insight fitted in with the experimental facts that we have cited here. But much more than this, with the aid of some further discussion (which we need not go into here) he was able to show that it implied a new notion of the measure of time and space. Whereas in the Newtonian theory this measure had been taken as absolute and independent of all observers, Einstein's insight led to the conclusion that this measure has to be regarded as relative to the speed of the observer. Of course, this implied a radical change in many of the most fundamental concepts of physics. And as is now very well known, from these new concepts, with the aid of certain simple and reasonable further hypotheses, he was able to draw a wide range of inferences, many of a highly novel character, which have thus far withstood the test of experiment and observation.

It is important to point out, in this connection, that the older form of Newtonian insight has never been definitely disproved.

Thus, working more or less at the same time as Einstein did, Lorentz proposed certain hypotheses about a material medium called "the ether," which was supposed to fill all space and to carry electromagnetic waves. In this way, using Newtonian conceptions of time and space, he was able to arrive at essentially the same mathematical predictions as those following from Einstein's theory. Nevertheless, Lorentz's theory was dropped, mainly because it was felt (evidently on grounds that are essentially aesthetic in nature) that the full set of hypotheses needed for such an ether theory were complicated, arbitrary, unnatural, ugly, etc. So we see once again that simple correspondence or non-correspondence with experimental facts can test hypotheses but not theories.

## Rational insight and rational fancy

It is clear from the preceding discussion that creative and original insight in science is intimately bound up, not only with the formation of new kinds of mental images, but also with new sorts of *rational insight*. For, evidently, discoveries of fundamentally new ways of looking at the whole world, such as those arising in the work of Newton and of Einstein, depend very strongly on the perception of the relevance of certain key questions, which help point to some contradictory or confused features of previously accepted general ways of thinking. The fresh insight into the general nature of things taking place in the "moment of understanding" is then unfolded or displayed both in the imagination (new mental images) and in the appearance of new lines of discursive reasoning which are free of the contradiction and confusion that was previously present.

It is evident, then, that we have to consider the relationship between imagination and reason if we wish to obtain an adequate account of the operation of the process of thought. Since we have here departed somewhat from the lines of Coleridge in our inquiry into imagination, it will now be necessary to do so again in our inquiry into rationality. So we should not expect to arrive at exactly the same role for reason as that suggested by Coleridge (though, of course, there will still be some rough parallel between our notion of rational insight and Coleridge's notion of reason).

A relevant indication of how we may understand what is to be meant by reason or rationality can be obtained by considering the origin of these words in the Latin "ratio." This would suggest that when we see the reason for something, we are aware of a totality of interrelated ratios or properties of that thing. But, of course, the sense of the word "ratio" is not restricted to relationships of numerical proportions, e.g.:

$$\frac{A}{B} = \frac{C}{D}$$

Rather, it also includes "qualitative proportions" such as "A is to B as C is to D" (to be expressed more succinctly as A : B :: C : D).

For example, the ancient Greeks had the view that heavenly matter is more perfect than earthly matter, and that it expressed the perfection of its nature by movement in a circle, which was regarded as the most perfect of all possible forms. This reasoning is implicitly based on the analogical ratio or proportion: "Heavenly matter is to earthly matter as the ideal of aesthetic and moral perfection of human behavior is to ordinary, everyday, imperfect human behavior."

Through such a "ratio" one was able to obtain an explanation of the whole cosmic order. But, of course, it is now well known that this sort of explanation did not work very well. Modern science ultimately came to a radically different mechanical type of explanation, in the development of which Newton's insight of universal gravitation played a key part. But now we can see that this insight had to be displayed not only *imaginatively* (through the image of an object that falls and yet never reaches the earth), but also *discursively*. The discursive display was, in this case, essentially an expression of a "ratio" that was implicitly present in the original flash of perception. Put in an ordinary verbal form, this was: as the successive positions of the falling apple are related, so are those of the falling moon, and so are those of any falling material object. Or, to state it more precisely, if A,B are the successive positions of the apple, C,D those of the moon, E,F those of any other object, then:

$$A : B :: C : D :: E : F$$

Because this ratio applies both to all actual objects and to all possible objects, it is *universal* and *necessary* (in the sense that it could not be otherwise). It is thus a *law*, which expresses rational harmony that is expected to prevail in all aspects of natural process.

More generally, all our concepts and explanations (whether of universal and necessary character or not) have at their core the perception of a totality of ratios or proportions, certain essential aspects of which may be displayed discursively in the way described above. Thus, to perceive such a simple thing as the straightness of a line is to see that each segment of it is related to the next segment, as the next is in turn related to the one that follows it. Or, in more concise terms, if $S_1$, $S_2$, $S_3$, denote any three successive segments, then $S_1 : S_2 :: S_2 : S_3$. If, however, the line should suddenly change its direction, at a certain point, then we would see that the segment that precedes this point is not related to the one that follows in the same way as prevails among the rest of the segments. If we could introduce the symbol X to mean 'is not to' then, for this case, we could write $S_1$ X $S_2 :: S_2 : S_3$ (i.e., $S_1$ is not to $S_2$, as $S_2$ is to $S_3$).

When we are perceiving one line meeting another, we are immediately aware of a totality of such similarities and differences of ratio. And, of course, as our attention goes to more complex structures of lines and surfaces forming a geometrical figure, we begin to be aware of a whole hierarchy of such ratios and their relationships. This hierarchy can develop indefinitely in its complexity and subtlety, as our perception extends into every phase of life. No matter what we perceive, however, the essential meaning or content of this perception involves a totality of ratio, in the most general sense of this word.

It cannot be emphasized too strongly that the apprehension of this totality of ratio takes place in an act of insight, within which the whole content is implicit or enfolded. As has already been pointed out, the first unfolding or display of this insight is in the form of an image. Within this image, the precise specification of the various ratios or proportions is evidently still mainly implicit (as relationships of various features of the form). But then, a bit later, through discursive thought and language, certain essential features of the totality of ratio are displayed explicitly as well. It is only when this has happened that the mind is fully ready for the content of an insight to pass into the domain of fancy or constructive thought.

In such fancy or constructive thought, a qualitatively different process takes place. Here, we begin, not only with already available images in the manner indicated earlier, but also with already available concepts consisting of structures of ratio or proportion logically arranged in ways that come mainly from memory. And so, we are led to distinguish between *imaginative and rational insight*, which is the primary act of perception through the mind, along with its immediate display, and *imaginative and rational fancy*, which is the construction or putting together of known concepts and images in a logical order.

An extreme case of rational fancy arises when a theory is *axiomatized*. In axiomatizing a theory, we select a certain set of basic concepts along with their relationships as expressed verbally or mathematically; and from these we aim to derive all the significant consequences of the theory in question, through a process of logical inference. Of course, as has been indicated earlier, every mental process must contain the two sides of insight and fancy together, though in each particular step there may be more emphasis on one side or the other. Thus, in axiomatizing a theory, we need a certain insight to select suitable axioms and to draw certain inferences from them, but evidently this insight does not generally extend to novel and original perceptions, such as those of Newton and Einstein, in which new kinds of images and new ways of thinking about the world as a whole first emerged into view.

The process of axiomatization is often very useful in facilitating certain lines of application of a theory. In addition, it can play a key role in making new discoveries possible. For example, geometrical insight was first axiomatized in the work of Euclid. This led to further work, which ultimately demonstrated certain arbitrary features of Euclidean geometry. This demonstration ultimately proved to be the key clue pointing to the possibility of new non-Euclidean forms of geometry. These latter generally had features not fitting in with the ordinary intuition of space as derived from general experience and sense perception. So the axiomatization of geometry helped lead to new insights. And it was able to do this mainly because the extreme precision of expression of the axioms make possible the detection of certain contradictory, confused, and arbitrary features of common and ordinary ideas about space.

In more modern approaches to mathematics, the meanings of the basic axiomatic concepts are often left fairly free, so that they are often determined mainly by the way in which the axioms are related. This is evidently a move toward emphasizing the side of creative and original insight. It corresponds to the possibility envisaged by Coleridge of permitting the basic images of imaginative fancy to be considerably altered so as to allow the total construction to reach a greater degree of harmony. But of course, such a mode of thought is still primarily a development of rational and imaginative fancy, rather than an act of creative insight, in which a new totality of images and ratios are perceived as a single, harmonious whole, first implicit and enfolded, and then explicit and unfolded.

The axiomatization of theories has, however, also had some negative effects in the development of modern science. What has happened is that when a theory has been given a more or less axiomatic form, the resulting appearance of precision, fixity, and perfect logical order has often given rise to the impression that knowledge has finally arrived at a kind of ultimate truth. And so the axiomatic form can act as a set of "blinkers" preventing people from looking in new directions, rather than as a set of hints and clues pointing to contradictions and inadequacies in existing lines of thought.

Indeed, the emphasis on the axiomatic mode of thinking tends to lead modern physicists to look on the development of precise mathematical formulations of law, along with detailed mathematical predictions of experimental results, as the main end of research in physics, while insight and perception through the mind are regarded as little more than incidental means of achieving such an end.

The whole matter is thus turned upside down. Rational and imaginative fancy are taken as the base, or the deep foundation and substructure, of our knowledge, while rational and imaginative insight are, at least tacitly and often explicitly as well, taken as a relatively superficial structure which works from this base. And so it is not seen that the deep origin of our general lines of thinking is in creative and original acts of insight, the content of which is then further unfolded and developed in the domain of fancy, ultimately to serve as hints or clues which help to indicate or point to new acts of insight, and thus to complete the cycle of the process of knowledge.

## The parallelism between intelligence and the process of thought

As has already been indicated, terms such as imagination, reason, and thought are being used in a somewhat different sense in this essay from that in which they were used by authors such as Coleridge and Hegel. Such a difference is, perhaps, inevitable. For in the nature of the case, this sort of term cannot be given a precise denotation, so that if we look at the subject in a different way we will have to use words differently, to indicate the meaning that we have in mind.

In my view, the clearest way of considering the overall operation of the mind is through inquiry into the distinction between intelligence and thought. I propose that the word "intelligence" commonly signifies a kind of mental alertness which is in essence a sort of perception. In the primary act of insight, which, for example, takes place in a flash of understanding, we *see* (though, evidently, not through the senses) a whole range of differences, similarities, connections, disconnections, totalities of universal and particular ratio or proportion, and so forth. This insight, which is of the essential quality of intelligence, cannot ultimately be a mere product of memory and training, because in each case it has to be seen anew. Rather, it is an act of *perception through the mind* (essentially what was called "nous" by the ancient Greeks). As such, it is a particular case of perception as a whole. This latter includes not only perception through the mind, but also sense perception, aesthetic perception, and emotional perception (perception through feelings).

It seems clear that the totality of perception cannot appropriately be analyzed further, or traced back to some yet more fundamental faculty. Rather, this perception is itself a primary act. Of course, we can analyze certain details concerning how the organs of perception (e.g. the eye) work, and how the nerves connect these organs to various functions in the brain. But this is in no sense an analysis of *perception itself*. Rather, before we can even make such an analysis we have to take for granted the operation of intelligence or perception through the mind. Without this, such an analysis would have no meaning. For how can the intelligence needed to perceive the meaning of this analysis be itself perceived and compared with what is implied by the analysis?

Nor is it appropriate to try to identify perception *in its totality* with some particular faculty, such as imagination or reason. For, after all, the meaning of the word "imagination" must ultimately be restricted in some way by its implicit reference to the power to make mental images. And the meaning of the word "reason" is similarly restricted in some way by its reference to the power to develop discursive displays of "ratio" or rational thought. In my view, both Coleridge and Hegel tend to put something rather limited in its implications, such as imagination or reason, into the place for the primary source of creation and origination in the human being as a whole. I would rather suggest that the act of perception, considered as a totality which is not yet differentiated, is closer to this source. For the origin of this act must evidently be intrinsically unknown and indefinable, not capable of being attributed to some particular faculty that may be involved in perception. (This means, of course, that perception in its totality could not ultimately be explained or accounted for in terms of any theory, scientific or otherwise, because each theory is itself a form of insight, and therefore merely a particular and special kind of perception.)

The other side of the operation of mind is indicated by the word "thought." Considering that this word now refers to what in Coleridge's terms would be called "the pole of mental process opposite to intelligence," we note that, in thought, the aspects of recurrence, repetition, identity, and stability are what is given a primary emphasis. The roots of thought are indeed indicated by all the uses of the prefix "re," which means "to turn around" and "to come back again." Thus, the eternal recurrence of day and night, or of the seasons, must make a deep impression on the mind of man. Long before he could consciously think of the subject, the whole operation of the mind must have become stably attuned to this recurrence, so that, for example, the expectation of the following of day and night on each other became a fixed feature of his mental processes. Similarly, when men continually repeated certain operations, conscious or otherwise, these became fixed in their minds as habitual reactions. Indeed, even the most abstract operations carried out today, such as those used in mathematics, soon result in similar reactions, so that a skilled mathematician has a great deal of his knowledge "at his fingertips" in a form that requires little or no conscious attention. So, in all these ways, man's thinking process slowly came into being and formed itself into what may be called *reactive thought*.

Reactive thought works quite well as long as experience does not go too far outside the context in which such thought developed. But, sooner or later, something is bound to happen with which the existing pattern of reactive thought cannot deal adequately. A very elementary example can be obtained by considering a young child who finds bright objects pleasing and develops a reaction of reaching for them. This is evidently an elementary type of reactive thought, in the sense that the reaction includes a kind of knowledge from experience that bright objects are pleasing objects. But now suppose that the child reaches for a fire and burns himself. Immediately the reaction is powerfully inhibited. The next time the child sees a bright object he may react toward it, but this reaction will now be associated with an inhibiting movement based on the memory of the painful feeling. So the outgoing energy is held back and directed inward. It is such a reversal of energy direction that is the beginning of a process of *reflective thought*. This moves mainly within the nervous system, seeking a solution of the problem which is, in this case, to enjoy bright objects without being burned by them.

Now every outgoing impulse has a structure that corresponds at least in some rough way to the object toward which it is directed. When this impulse is reflected or turned back, it will stimulate the sensory nerves in ways similar to how they would be stimulated by the object itself. Thus, some kind of *image* is created in the nervous system, which can be perceived along with the object, or even when the object is not immediately in the field of perception. Such an image is not merely some idle fancy arising passively out of memory in the stream of consciousness. Rather, it is actively produced by the reflection of the outgoing impulses, and is therefore systematically related to the problem or difficulty that led to the reflection in the first place. So, in the internal process thus set in movement, it is possible to seek a combination of thoughts that resolves the difficulty, first in relation to the image (i.e. in the imagination) and later in relation to the actual fact.

Evidently, then, reflection is in the first instance a way of meeting some difficulty by constantly changing the pattern of reactive thought to adapt it better to the actual fact. The primary function of such reflective thought is thus to try to re-establish a state of stability and equilibrium in which reactive thought is once again adequate to meet the situation in which we find ourselves. Indeed, once reflection encounters a pattern that gives a solution, then, sooner or later, as this pattern is repeated, it is absorbed into the whole body of reactive thought. We shall thus say that thought of this kind is to be characterized as *reactive–reflective* (indicating that reaction is what is primary in this polarity, in the sense that reflection is mainly a means of adjusting or adapting a basically reactive pattern).

From the above it is clear that as we approach the extreme in

which reactive thought is the principal factor in mental operation, the process will tend to become mainly mechanical. What
characterizes a mechanical process is a certain kind of repetitive-
ness. That is to say, its essential feature is that when left to itself it
moves according to a law of inertia (i.e. of the necessity for a
certain property of motion to continue to repeat indefinitely until
the system is disturbed from outside). Reactive thought
evidently moves with such an inertia, which arises largely
through associative links that are established in a habitual
pattern by repetition of a series of similar mental and physical
operations. This sort of pattern tends to change mainly when
external circumstances alter, and force thought to react in a
different way. It is thus clear that reactive thought is in essence a
mechanical process.

Reactive thought is, of course, necessary, because without it
we would have to reflect on every step. Very often this would be
much too slow (for example, when driving a motor car). And
besides, the totality of steps is generally so great that we could
not reflect on all of them at once. So even though it is basically
mechanical, reactive thought is an essential side or aspect of the
process of thought as a whole. Nevertheless, *unless there is an
opportunity for reflective thought to respond beyond the framework of
such a mechanical mode of operation*, thought as a whole will
inevitably entangle itself in a growing mass of problems and
difficulties that it cannot resolve.

We can see, however, that as ordinarily carried out, even the
response of reflective thought tends rather easily to fall under
the domination of a mechanical pattern. Thus, the attempt to
solve a problem often does not go beyond the mere search of
memory patterns to try to discover one that will provide a solution. In the long run this will result in little more than a
repetition of memory patterns on a new level. That is, instead of
having an *immediate reaction* dominated by a memory pattern, we
will have a reflection, leading to a *delayed reaction* dominated by a
memory pattern. The delayed pattern may be richer and more
subtle than the original pattern, but it is nonetheless basically
mechanical.

The next higher stage of thought arises when there is a
problem for the solution of which it is seen that no memory
pattern is available. What happens then is that the mind tries to
"figure out" what to do. Generally, this process tends mainly to
involve imaginative and rational fancy. That is, by ordering and

arranging available images and concepts in new ways, as well as by adapting or modifying such images and concepts, the mind may arrive at a solution. As pointed out earlier, a certain insight is involved in such a process. Yet it is clear that in the long run what can be done in this way is rather strictly limited by the total set of basic images and concepts that may happen to be available. Thus, ultimately this sort of process must at best remain within frontiers determined in a basically mechanical way.

In a wide range of contexts, however, the response of rational and imaginative fancy is limited much more seriously than would be implied by the mere fixing of certain frontiers beyond which it cannot go. What happens further is that reflective thought allows its basic mode of operation to be dominated by the apparent need to provide a solution that would fit in with the vast background of already existent reactive thought patterns. Now what is characteristic of such reactive thought patterns is a certain grossness and crudeness—an inability to respond sensitively and freely in new ways to subtle indications of significant changes in the observed fact. For, after all, a reaction is such that either it works in its general accustomed way or else it doesn't work at all. So when reflective thought is dominated by the attempt to find a solution that would fit in with the background of already existent reactive thought, it inevitably commits itself to imitating these crude and gross patterns of response. *The main way in which it does this is overemphasizing the hard and fast definition of logical categories.*

For example, a child may suffer a violent adverse reaction to a certain kind of food. When he reflects on this, he may incorporate this reaction into his conscious thought by thinking: "*All* food of this nature is bad." By implication, this constitutes a precise and fixed distinction between all food similar to that which disturbed him and all food different from that which disturbed him. Behind this implication is the general notion: "Either a particular item of food is in the 'disturbing' category or it is not, and that is *all* that is possible." Such a lumping of things into opposing and sharply defined and fixed categories evidently corresponds very well with the reactions that give rise to this line of reflective thought. This fit between reflection and reaction then permits a solution of the problem, in the form of the development of a fixed response of keeping away from foods of a "disturbing" nature.

It must be pointed out that man's discovery of the rules of

formal logic (e.g. a thing is either *A* or not *A*) constituted an important step forward. Such rules were necessary in a wide range of contexts in which they were appropriate (i.e. those in which simple and sharp distinctions can consistently be made). Nevertheless, this very same development also led man into a dangerous and destructive trap. Thus, for example, while it might be appropriate to divide all objects of a certain kind as being either inside or outside a certain region of space, it is generally inappropriate and even harmful to divide all types of food in this simple way, between "disturbing" and "non-disturbing." For the reasons why food may cause a disturbance are quite complex and may have to do with all sorts of factors, going outside the question of whether the food is of one type or another.

Yet, as long as the mind is dominated by the background of reactive thought patterns, reflective thought will tend automatically and mechanically to respond in all cases indiscriminately with some sharp and unalterably fixed formal logical distinction in the manner described above. (An extreme case of this arises in a hostile reaction to people of another race, to which reflective thought responds with prejudicial judgements such as: "People are divided into mutually exclusive races and all people of this particular race are bad.")

How, then, can thought respond to a problem or a difficulty without being dominated by an irrelevant, confusing, and generally destructive mechanical pattern of reaction? Evidently, what is needed for this is a quality of insight going beyond any particular fixed form of reaction and associated reflective thought. *This insight must be free of conditioning to previously existing patterns, otherwise it will, of course, ultimately be just an extension of mechanical reaction.* Rather, it has to be fresh and new, creative and original.

As indicated earlier, insight of this kind is a form of perception through the mind, which is the essence of what is most deeply meant by the word "intelligence." When such intelligence operates, then in each case there is a perception of where the ever-changing dividing line between a given pair of opposing categories properly falls, and of whether a given pair of such categories is relevant. So the mind is no longer dominated by its mechanical tendency to hold unalterably to such fixed and limited sets of categories, nor by the automatic reactions that have ultimately given rise to the tendency to hold unalterably to such fixed and limited sets of categories. And thus whenever there is a difficult problem, the mind is able, if necessary, to drop the old categories and to create new forms of rational and imaginative insight, which now serve to guide thought along the new lines that may be necessary for resolving the problem.

It is implicitly accepted in a large part of our common notions on the subject, however, that intelligence is an extension or development from thought. That is, thought is regarded as providing a sort of base or ground from which intelligence arises, and on which in turn it operates. *It cannot be too strongly emphasized that what is being suggested here is that intelligence does not thus arise primarily out of thought.* Rather, as pointed out earlier, the deep source of intelligence is the unknown and indefinable totality from which all perception originates.

Clearly, then, intelligence is not to be regarded as a result of accumulated knowledge which could be learned, for example, as a science or as a technique. Rather, it can perhaps best be regarded as an *art*—the art of perception through the mind. Such an art requires great insight and skill. When these are absent, thought quickly gets lost in confusion.

There can be no system or specifiable method for avoiding the tendency for thought to fall into such confusion. Rather, what is required is a general alertness which makes us aware, from moment to moment, of how the process of thought is getting caught in fixed sets of categories. However, even such alertness does not provide for perfect harmony in this unceasing movement. Nevertheless, with the right quality of mental energy, insight, and skill, the art of intelligent perception will enable us sooner or later to meet whatever difficulties may arise, without getting lost in the fixity of categories that leads to irresolvable confusion. And so it may perhaps be said that it is just in such creative perception of disharmony in the process of thought, that man may come upon the deepest harmony that is open to him.

## NOTE

1　Barfield, Owen (1971) *What Coleridge Thought*. Middletown: Wesleyan University Press, pp. 76, 128; and Wallace, W. (1904) *The Logic of Hegel*. London: Oxford University Press, pp. 92, 379.

# 4

# THE ART OF PERCEIVING MOVEMENT

In this essay we shall inquire into the functioning of language and thought. Such an inquiry is necessary primarily because over the ages thought and language have developed in a form that is by now mainly one of *fragmentation*. Of course, there is a real need for thought and language momentarily to focus attention on one thing or another, as the occasion demands. But when each such thing is regarded as separately existent and essentially independent of the broader context of the whole in which it has its origin, its sustenance, and its ultimate dissolution, then one is no longer merely focusing attention, but, rather, one is engaged in breaking the field of awareness into disjoint parts, whose deep unity can no longer be perceived.

Such supposedly fragmentary aspects of human endeavor as art and science correspond to our consideration of society as a set of separately existent nations, races, or political, economic, and religious groups. But all these parts are actually intimately related and interdependent, as aspects of an unbroken totality, which ultimately merges with the whole of existence. The idea that they are essentially separate and independent has brought about a continual series of crises throughout the whole of recorded history, but in recent times such crises have become sharper and more urgent.

Human existence, and, indeed, perhaps the very existence of any form of life at all on the surface of the earth, is now threatened by the development of technically advanced means of destruction. Even if there is no such universal destruction, mankind is confronted with a series of difficulties that may, in the long run, prove to be almost as severe. Thus, because of our generally fragmentary way of perceiving, experiencing, and acting, the world is faced with overpopulation, exhaustion of natural resources, pollution of the general environment, and interference with the ecological balance of life over the planet as a whole. And beyond this, such a mode of living is leading to an ever more meaningless social structure, in which we experience the very patterns of relationship that we ourselves have created as something separate from us and alien to what is deepest and most essential in each individual human being.

There is currently a fairly widespread realization of the existence of these dangers, and many groups are trying to take measures to deal with the ever-mounting series of apparently unsolvable problems with which human society is beset. Unfortunately, however, most of these attempts are aimed, as it were, very downstream at the *results* of fragmentation, and not at its origin in our mode of thinking and using language. This concentration on results has come about to a considerable extent because these modes of thinking and using language *are not at all easy to observe*. Indeed, they operate in very subtle ways, of which we are largely unaware, to interfere with proper attention by preventing us from seeing how things are interrelated, in ever-broader contexts.

Consider, for example, the question of establishing a proper ecological balance. This demands that the entire world with all human activity be considered as one undivided and unbroken whole. If, without their knowing it, the people who study ecology and try to apply their knowledge of it are themselves committed to their own personal interests, or to the interests of their own economic, political, social, or national groups, how can they allow the whole to be first in their thoughts? Inevitably, there will be subliminal pressures and tendencies to think in a fragmentary way that would seem to be appropriate to what is believed to be the overwhelming necessity of putting personal or group interests first. Thus, it will not be possible intelligently to think of and talk about all aspects that are relevant to the totality of the ecological cycles of the planet.

Similarly, we may consider what may be called the "totality of the ecological cycles" of society and the individual. In these cycles, man's thought and language may thus be regarded as a kind of "mental pollution" which generally prevents us from acting in a sensible or useful way. What, then, is the value of calls to political, social, or economic action, when we are unable to give proper attention to what we are doing because our minds are in a state of chaos through looking at everything, including ourselves, in a fragmentary way?

## On the reality of thought

If our troubles originate in a kind of "ocean" of thought and language, in which we are submerged, but of which we are only dimly aware, it would seem reasonable to begin immediately to inquire into the actual function of our thought and language. To do this requires, of course, that we give this function our serious attention. We do give such attention to a vast range of things, including nature, technology, politics, economics, society, psychological problems, and so forth. Why should thought and language be the one field left to function automatically and mechanically, without serious attention, so that the resulting confusion vitiates most of what we try to do in all other fields?

The first step in giving proper attention to thought and language depends on seeing that *thought is real*. Its reality can in fact be demonstrated by instruments such as the electro-encephalograph. These show that there is no thought without electrical and chemical changes, muscular tensions, and so forth. But the very same activity that is revealed on one side through such instruments is seen on the other side as *meaningful function*, both inward and outward. (The inward aspect is thought, imagination, etc., while the outward aspect is language, communication, practical activity, etc.) Houses, tables, chairs, cars, roads, farms, factories, and, indeed, almost all that we see in everyday life are thus extensions of thought. Nature may be regarded as that which takes shape by itself, while human activity leads to the creation of artifacts, shaped by human participation in natural process, ordered and guided by thought.

The real and indeed pivotal role of thought in determining not only the structure of the environment that man has created, but, even more, the general stability (or instability) of his society, can usefully be compared to that of DNA in the living organism. As is well known, biologists have discovered that the hereditary characteristics of such organisms are determined by very long and complex DNA molecules having the form of a double spiral. When a cell divides, the molecule is "copied," and thus the "information" needed to order the growth and structuring of the new cells is carried along. Moreover, "wrong" features of the DNA molecule (for instance, pieces of virus DNA which are accidentally incorporated into the cell's DNA) may also be copied, to the detriment of future generations of cells.

Similarly, we may say that in communication, each person's brain "copies" the thought of the other, sometimes faithfully, and sometimes with "wrong" features that tend to impede further communication and thinking. This replication of thought patterns is of crucial importance in all that we make and in all that we do, both individually and socially. Indeed, if we suddenly lost all memory of our thought patterns, society would collapse, and the individual would cease to be able to survive, since nobody would know how he is supposed to be related to other people, nor even how to take care of his own needs. And evidently, the tendency to go on copying wrong or inappropriate thought patterns must lead to an accumulation of problems, both social and individual, that cannot be solved unless these patterns cease to be copied in this way.

One may pursue this analogy further, by considering the occasional mutations of DNA molecules, to give rise to new forms of living organisms. Biologists generally suppose that these mutations come about mainly or perhaps entirely by chance, and that only those mutations leading to organisms that are suitably adapted to the environment will survive. Similarly, man's thought can and does change, either by chance or otherwise. Through such changes, his thought can in principle become better adapted to his actual environment. However, unlike what happens in the cell, a man does not necessarily have to die if his thought is not properly adapted in this way. Rather, as we have already indicated, he can give attention to his thought, to see whether it fits the reality in which he lives, and he can experiment, so as to change it, if it does not fit.

It we are to be able thus to attend to our thought we have, however, to be aware of it *as such*; that is, as a real movement that is actually going on, both inwardly and outwardly, with real effects of very widespread and deep significance that interpenetrate and ultimately merge with the whole of the reality in which we live. We cannot do this if we go on with the prevailing tendency to concentrate almost exclusively on the problems which are the *results* of our thinking process, and thus fragment these results from their origin in the thought that automatically and habitually "copies" inappropriate patterns. If we fail in this way to give proper attention to the origin of our problems, then the very thought that is aimed at solving them will be of the same fragmentary and confused nature as that which is producing them, so that what we do will tend to make things worse, rather than better.

## On the fragmentation between the content of thought and its function

One of the main reasons why we actually find it very difficult to attend to our thought and its overall function as a real movement in the way indicated in the previous section, is that our notions concerning the general nature of thought are themselves fragmentary and confused. This confusion begins very early in life. At a certain age (as observed by Piaget, that of development from relatively immediate and direct sensory motor thought to more abstract symbolization of thought, in terms of language) the child often tends to suppose the *content* of his thought (for instance, imaginary objects) to be as real as things that can be seen or touched. Eventually he discovers, of course, that such content is only "imaginary," and thus he comes to regard it as "unreal." A young child is, however, probably not yet ready to understand something much more subtle, which is crucially important in this regard. This is that, while the content of thought may be either "real" or "unreal," its function is nevertheless *always* real. This function is, first, to give meaning and shape to perception by calling attention to what is regarded as relevant or essential in the context of interest and, second, to give rise to feelings and urges that promote actions appropriate to the context, i.e. it contains what may be called *motivation*.

As an example, one may consider a table. One may think of it as a supporter of paper or as an obstacle in the way of where one wishes to go. Each of these ways of thinking leads one to see the table in a different form of perception, which calls attention to different aspects and in this way gives rise to different motivations as to what to do about the table (either to write on it or to push it aside). *We thus emphasize that thought and the perceptions that guide action, along with the feelings and urges that constitute the motivation for such action, are inseparable aspects of one whole movement, and that to try to regard them as separately existent is a form of fragmentation between the content of thought and its overall function.*

To fragment the content of thought from its overall function in the way described above leads to very serious confusion in action and in human relationships in general. For example, the thought of the inferiority of human beings belonging to different nations or ethnic groups and having different customs leads one to *see* such people as inferior beings and to feel the motivation to treat them in a manner that would be fitting to their supposed inferiority. One tends to fall into this sort of confused response because one fails to see the content of thought and its function as a single unbroken flow. Rather, one tends first to concentrate exclusively on the content (the notion of inferiority of people who differ from oneself), which is seen as "merely a thought" and therefore unreal or perhaps "only a mental reality" and therefore not very important. Then, when one experiences the in-built function of this thought by "actually seeing" other people as inferior, and by "actually feeling" the urge or motive to treat them as such, he loses sight of the content in which this function originated, and thinks: "This is not just a mental image, but it is something real, something that I see and feel as an actual fact, which is very important and very urgent in its implications." So, it seems that the inferiority of these people has been proved and is not a "mere thought."

But, of course, this "proof" is illusory and the illusion is able to get by because of the fragmentation between the content of thought and its function. Behind this fragmentation is the implicit assumption (of which one is generally almost entirely unaware) that if one has a sense of experiencing something in perception and in one's inner feelings, this is necessarily "a mere thought." As has been indicated earlier, however, such a conclusion overlooks the fact that thought itself is real and has a real function in perception, motivation, and action, which operates very pervasively in almost all that we do.

When we fail to see this, the single unbroken movement in which the content of thought gives rise to a total function, is perceived and experienced as fragmented into two disjoint parts. One of these appears to be "merely thought" and the other seems to be some very widespread and extremely significant reality, external and internal, which originates outside of thought. In this way, the overall meaning of what is going on when thought takes place is deeply misunderstood.

A proper response to thought is in fact possible only when attention is an unbroken whole, and this requires that the content of thought and its overall function shall actually be seen and felt as a single undivided movement. As has been indicated earlier, our general inability to do this arises mainly in the difficulty that the young child has in learning to relate the abstract symbolization of thought in terms of language to direct sensory motor experience. Indeed, it is probable that when man was first developing abstract thought in terms of language he encountered a similar difficulty; and so the older generation was, at each stage, incapable of helping the younger generation out of its confusion on this score. In this way, the tendency to misunderstand the overall meaning of thought has been passed on from very early times until the present.

It is important to emphasize here that in developing abstract thought in terms of language man was not merely adding the use of signs and words to the rest of his activities. Rather, this development set in movement a far-reaching and deep change in man's way of giving attention and of being generally aware of the reality in which he lives. The essence of this change can be described as the introduction of the *symbolic function of language*. This includes not only the activity of a language symbol in evoking a whole range of meanings, but also its ability to call up a totality of feelings, urges, motivations, reactions, and reflexes which follow on these meanings. For example, a red light not only means "stop," but to a driver the perception of this symbol directly gives rise to all the mental, emotional, and physical reactions that are involved in *actually* stopping. Or, on a more abstract level, we may consider the musician or the mathematician who has assimilated a certain structure of abstract symbolic thoughts so thoroughly that it is "at his fingertips" in a skillful function, leaving his attention free to focus on the meaning of what he is doing.

So the main function of a language symbol is not to *stand for* or *represent* an object to which it corresponds. Rather, it initiates a total movement of memory, imagery, ideas, feelings, and reflexes, which serves *to order attention to and direct action* in a new mode that is not possible without the use of such symbols. Thus, when man generally failed to observe how these symbols actually functioned in the way described above, he fell into a widespread and deep confusion that interfered with proper attention and awareness in every aspect of his life.

The crucial importance of this confusion around the symbolic function of abstract thought in terms of language can be indicated by considering the role of this function in producing the conflicts that have led so persistently throughout the course of human history to hatred, violence, and general destruction. Very frequently, such behavior has been attributed to some ingrained feature of human nature. Indeed, more recently this sort of argument has been further justified by pointing out that animals are violent too, and thus the inference is drawn that human violence is a natural inheritance from man's animal ancestry. But, of course, such an argument ignores essential differences between animal conflicts and human violence. Thus, when animals of the same species fight (for instance, over a mate) this is seldom, if ever, carried to the point of killing. Instead, the loser simply walks away and ceases to be concerned about the whole affair. On the other hand, when human beings fight, this generally does not happen. Rather, the conflict is continued indefinitely (sometimes even for hundreds of years) as a result of man's talking and thinking about what has happened.

It seems ironical that man's thought and language, whose deep aim is to make possible rational communication and constructive action, have been a principal factor making for the indefinite continuation of irrational hatred and destructive violence. In essence, this has come about because man has not been able to perceive the operation of the symbolic function of language. For example, when those who lose a war say (and think) "How unjustly we have been treated!," they do not see the in-built function, which inevitably gives rise to feelings of self-pity, and the desire for revenge. Instead, as pointed out earlier in connection with the discussion of the thought of inferiority of people of other races, they suppose that such feelings arise "in the depth of the soul" and are therefore of supreme significance (even to the point of requiring the sacrifice of all in order that "right shall be done"). But if man could see language and its symbolic function as a single unbroken movement it would be evident that the feelings in question are arising mechanically out of thought, and therefore have little significance.

In a certain abstract sense, the point is in fact already understood by almost everyone. This is shown by the rhyme repeated by little children: "Sticks and stones may break my bones, but names can never hurt me!" The truth of the rhyme seems obvious. Yet few have been able consistently and throughout life as a whole to listen to someone who is insulting them without some sort of reaction that interferes with proper attention and rational thought.

This kind of reaction is in essence what occurs generally in the various forms of prejudice, and in the tendency for resentments, quarrels, and conflicts to go on almost indefinitely, interfering with proper function in most human activities and distorting human relationships at every level. What is not commonly understood is that such a reaction, leading to a response that is not in general intelligent or suitable to the actual situation, originates in the prevailing fragmentation between the content of thought and its overall function.

If this fragmentation is to come to an end, it is clearly necessary to inquire deeply into the actual function of our thought, not only as is commonly being done in scientific research, with the aid of electrical instruments and mathematical models, but, much more, through serious and sustained attention to one's own thoughts as they actually take place. For example, a scientist may experiment with instruments on the brain, but if his own thought and language share in the general fragmentation, he will be incapable of proper attention, and so he must inevitably come to confused, illusory, and deceptive results.

Each man has thus, from the very outset, to be aware of the generally inattentive mode of functioning of his own thought, which allows him automatically and habitually to go on "copying" a fragmentary structure that has been built up over the ages and passed down to us. Each of us can in this way see the fragmentary structure of thought *as such* as a real process with a real function in each individual and in society as a whole. We have then to inquire into the function, and to experiment with changes in it, which may lead to a different "mental DNA," free of the prevailing tendency toward fragmentation between the content of thought and its function, and thus more viable than the kind that we now have.

## On the necessary incompleteness of our world views

Is it really possible to give attention to thought and language in the way previously indicated? Would this not be equivalent to trying to make thought and language match themselves? And would this not be a confused or contradictory notion?

If we were to imagine that thought and language were some definite and well-defined sort of thing which could in principle be known completely (or in ever-greater degrees of approximation), then we would indeed be falling into some kind of confusion. How, indeed, could the content of thought possibly have within it a complete account of its own total structure and function? However, if we notice that thought and language are like any other aspect of reality, we will not expect such complete knowledge. As with every other real function, thought and language require ever-fresh attention and observation to test our existent knowledge.

However, the notion of the necessary incompleteness of our knowledge runs counter to the commonly accepted scientific tradition, which has generally taken the form of supposing that science seeks to arrive ultimately at absolute truth, or at least at a steady approach to such truth, through a series of approxima-tions. This tradition has been maintained, in spite of the fact that the actual history of science fits much better into the notion of unending possibilities for new discoveries, approaching no visible limit or end. For example, classical physics, which held sway for several hundred years, has given way to relativity and quantum theory. These theories contain fundamentally new features, and are radically different in essence from classical physics. Of course, they do contain some features of the older theory, as limiting cases or approximations, and thus the latter is seen still to have a certain relative and limited validity. But, in turn, for every problem solved by relativity and quantum theory, several new and hitherto unsuspected problems have arisen. Indeed, physics is now in a state of flux, in which we expect the development of yet newer theories, again radically novel and different, in terms of which current theories will be seen as having only some relative and limited kind of validity. What has happened and is still happening in this respect suggests an indefinite and unending unfolding into a measureless unknown, rather than a better covering of some limited, measurable, and in principle completely knowable domain.

One of the most striking examples of such a development is to be seen in modern cosmology, which has changed radically and completely every ten years or so. For example, we now have "quasars," "pulsars," "black holes," and a number of other new basic concepts which were not even suspected a few years ago. It is rather ironical that, whereas a theory of the universe in its totality is just what ought never to change if it is true, theories of the cosmos have in fact changed faster than almost any other kind of theory. It would indeed be consistent with what has actu-ally been discovered thus far to suppose that the "universe in its totality" or "reality as a whole" is unknown, vast, and limitless in extent, depth, and subtlety. After all, the totality includes not only all that has been discovered about nature by all science, but also us, our language, our thoughts, feelings, and intelligent perceptions, and, indeed, all that we can ever come to discover, and very probably much more, beyond our capacity to imagine or conceive.

One would thus not suppose that to search for a complete theory of the universe is a meaningful or sensible thing to try to do. What, then, is the use of attempting to formulate theories that aim to cover the whole?

As indicated in the previous essay, it is useful in answering such a question to consider the original meaning of the Greek word "theoria," from which the modern word "theory" has come. This has the same root as "theater," in a verb, meaning "to view." This suggests that we might regard a theory as "a view," or "a form of insight," rather than as a "well-defined and certain knowledge about reality." Theories of the universe as a whole (as well as theories of the universal constitution or structure of matter) can then be regarded as furnishing overall world views.

Mankind has indeed always been constructing world views, beginning with early creation myths that attempt to explain the whole of his "world," and going on to more modern philosophical speculation and scientific theories. As man inquires and learns, he discovers that each of these world views is able to fit the reality in which he lives only in some limited way. So different and novel world views have continually to be created to keep up with man's ever-changing knowledge and experience.

What is significant in this regard is not merely the *content* of these various world views, but, much more, *their proper function*, which is to help organize man's ever-changing knowledge and experience in a coherent way. To limit our world views by regarding them as absolute truth or as stages of a steady approach to such a truth evidently interferes with their proper function, for this tends to prevent the consideration of fundamentally different notions that may be needed to fit new observations and experiences. Our world views have thus to be able to alter radically if this is called for by what we learn and by what we observe. To attempt to regard these views as permanently fixed or as steady stages in an advance toward an ultimate fixed truth is like putting a solid rock into a flowing stream; the result is turbulence and chaos. Rather, it can be said that our world views should "flow with" the stream of reality as we come into ever-changing contact with the latter.

One of the main reasons why we tend to find it difficult to allow such a "free flow" to take place is that, as indicated in the previous section, we are not generally aware that the thought in our world views is a real process that actually does have the organizing function described above. Rather, attention tends to concentrate almost exclusively on what appears to be the permanently fixed content of the world view, so that the organization of our overall knowledge actually produced in its functioning is tacitly attributed to "reality itself" or to "the way things are." And so the attitude toward the truth of theories that prevails in the current scientific tradition tends to lead us to fall unwittingly into the kind of fragmentation between the content of thought and its function that has been seen to be at the origin of most of the problems that mankind has faced over the ages, and still faces today.

Of course, what we are saying here is itself an aspect of a world view, and so we have to be alert and watchful to see that we do not fall into the above-described trap of tacitly identifying its content with some sort of absolute and final truth. To fail to give adequate attention in this way would lead us to fall back once again into the generally prevailing fragmentation between the content of thought and its function. And to do this would, of course, be of little value. For what can be the use of exchanging present forms of such fragmentation for new ones?

## On the primacy of movement and undivided wholeness, as implied by modern physics

As was indicated in the previous section, the current scientific tradition involves an attitude to knowledge which tends very strongly to lead to a fragmentation between the content of our thought and its overall function. In this regard, physics plays an especially important role, because physics is widely believed to be either the basis of other sciences, or else the source of a pattern toward which other sciences should aspire.

One of the extreme forms of the fragmentary approach in physics is to be seen in the commonly accepted notion that, at bottom, the world is constituted of a set of separately existent fundamental entities of a fixed nature (elementary particles) which serve as "basic building blocks" for the whole of reality.

But, as is implicit in the discussion given in the previous section, even this mode of thought in which analysis is carried to an extreme will not necessarily imply fragmentation if we do not identify its content with an absolute truth about reality as a whole. If, instead, we consider such a notion to be merely a "world view," then we can see that its proper function is to organize our present overall knowledge and experience in a generally coherent way, and not to make us believe that the whole of reality actually is constituted out of a collection of separately existent "building blocks." When we understand this we are free to take into account the fact that, while analysis of everything into a set of constituent particles was found to fit experience in physical research fairly well more or less until the end of the nineteenth century, it has failed to fit most of what has been learned in the twentieth century. And so we are able to see the need for development of a very different sort of world view.

To help indicate how our world view has to change, we first note that the atoms originally thought to be the basic "building blocks" have since been split into electrons, protons, and neutrons. But these so-called elementary particles have in turn been shown to have an as yet very poorly known deeper structure, and to be capable of transformation, allowing for the creation and annihilation of an apparently unlimited number of further new unstable particles of a similar nature. It is clear that these particles are very unlikely to be ultimate and basic building blocks either. Thus far, the search for such basic constituents has failed; and, indeed, the goal seems to retreat to the horizon each time that we think we are approaching it.

However, in spite of this failure there has been a sort of faith, widely accepted in current scientific research, that sooner or later such constituents must be discovered. This faith is probably based on a tacit conclusion that nothing else is possible but that the universe is constituted out of *some* kind of basic particles, and so it appears that the only real task is to discover just what the nature of these particles actually is.

In such a view, the notion of an ultimate set of particles constituting the whole universe seems to be no restriction on our way of thinking at all, because it appears that one has infinite freedom in the choice of properties that these particles might have. But, of course, it is a serious restriction in fact. One may understand something of the nature of this restriction by considering a man who is walking on a vast, practically limitless, planar surface and who concentrates his attention almost exclusively on a very complex system of paths along which he can continue to walk indefinitely, without noticing that he is limited in not being able in this way to look at what is above or below this surface. Similarly, by keeping one's mind narrowly focused on the limitless elaboration of complex paths of analytical thought about the supposed particle constitution of the whole of reality, one may easily lose sight of the fact that in this way one's attention never leaves the "plane" defined by the *particle concept as a whole*.

Even if we consider what is now known about the present so-called elementary particles, we can see that there are a number of important new developments, indicating that we have already to explore what is outside the "plane" of the particle concept as a whole. Thus, the theory of relativity shows that these "particles" cannot consistently be taken as the starting-point of our reasoning. Rather, they have to be understood as abstractions from a stream of events or a flow of process, in which *every* object is regarded as in essence a relatively invariant form of such abstraction. That is to say, an object is now considered to be more like a pattern of movement than like a solid separate thing that exists autonomously. Any localizable structure may be described as a "world tube," brought into existence in space and time from a broader background or context and eventually dissolving into the background.

Einstein, attempting to obtain a consistent description of a world tube, proposed that the universe be regarded as a field which is an unbroken and undivided whole. Particles are then treated as certain kinds of abstraction from the total field, notably, as localized regions in which the field is very intense. As one gets further from the center of such a region, the field gets weaker, until it merges imperceptibly with the fields of other particles. So there can be no question of isolating separately existent "building blocks," such as atoms or elementary particles.

In the quantum theory, it has been found that the observed object can no longer consistently be said to exist separately and independently of the experimental conditions. Rather, the form of the experimental conditions and the meaning of the experimental results have now to be one whole, in which analysis into autonomously existent elements is not relevant. What is meant here by wholeness could be indicated metaphorically by calling attention to a pattern, like that in a carpet. Insofar as what is relevant *is* the pattern, it has no meaning to say that different parts of such a pattern (e.g. various flowers and trees that are to be seen in it) are separate objects in interaction. Similarly, in the quantum context one can regard terms like "experimental conditions" and "observed object" as aspects of a single overall "pattern" that are, in effect, abstracted or "pointed out" by our mode of description. Thus, to think of an "observing instrument" interacting with a separately existent "observed particle" has no meaning.

In this way, Einstein's emphasis on undivided wholeness of the universe in terms of field is carried yet further. For even that which "observes" or "measures" the field can no longer consistently be regarded as something that exists separately from the field. In the context of these new theoretical developments, the notion of analyzability of the whole universe into "basic building blocks" is thus seen to be utterly irrelevant.

One can obtain a certain insight into the new world view implied in all this by considering the analogy of a moving fluid with relatively constant stable patterns of movement; consider a stream flowing past a bridge, producing vortices and stationary wave forms. Evidently, each vortex or stationary wave form is an abstraction of an ordered form of movement, which is centered in a certain region of space, but which actually involves the whole fluid. For example, two vortices may have different centers, but their patterns of movement ultimately merge in the fluid as a whole. At no place is there a division or break in the pattern of movement. Evidently, the notion of a division or a separation between vortices is at most a convenient abstraction, and is not a description of "what is."

Of course, scientists tend to say that fluid is really made of atoms, which are actually "separate building blocks" out of which the fluid is constituted. But as has been seen on a closer inspection, the atoms dissolve into a very poorly known, deeper structure that ultimately merges with the field of the whole universe. Indeed, even the instruments which observe the fluid are themselves composed of atoms and finer particles, which similarly merge in the universal field. And, going further still, we ourselves, with our brains and nervous systems, have a similar constitution. So, in a deep enough view, *we in our act of observation are like that which we observe*: relatively constant patterns abstracted from the universal field movement, and thus merging ultimately with all other patterns that can be abstracted from this movement.

We are led in this way to consider a very different world view from that which is behind classical physics. In this view, there is no ultimate set of separately existent entities, out of which all is supposed to be constituted. Rather, unbroken and undivided movement is taken as a primary notion. Or, equivalently, we can say: *What is* is a whole movement, in which each aspect flows into and merges with all other aspects. Atoms, electrons, protons, tables, chairs, human beings, planets, or galaxies are then to be regarded as abstractions from the whole movement and are to be described in terms of order, structure, and form in the movement. The notion of a separate substance or entity is dropped or, at most, retained as part of the earlier world view, which is now seen to fit the totality of our experience only in certain limited ways.

We are thus beginning to inquire into and explore the suggested new world view, in which movement is considered in the role of what is essential, without the need to suppose that there is something that is "doing the moving." It is just the automatic and habitual function of the earlier world view that leads us to try to *think* of this. *But it is important to emphasize that such a substance or entity is encountered only in thought, and is never found in reality.*

Scientists often experience difficulty with such notions. If there is no ultimate truth, they may ask, what is the meaning of scientific inquiry? Can there be a strong feeling for going on with such work? Isn't the search for knowledge of an ultimate truth what gives the scientist the drive behind his work? And then, if there is no ultimate substance or entity, what can it mean to talk about movement?

It is interesting to note that artists do not, as a rule, find these questions nearly so difficult. Thus, they generally seem to have a strong drive for doing their work, without regarding it as a source of ultimate truths. Moreover, many artists seem to understand the primary role of movement quite naturally and spontaneously. Thus, Leonardo da Vinci said (in a way that can be paraphrased a bit):

1   Movement gives shape to all forms.
2   Structure gives order to movement.

Evidently, this is close in meaning to what has been said here. Thus, the movement of the fluid is what gives shape to the form of a vortex. What gives order to this movement is a totality of structure, beginning with that of the surroundings in which the fluid moves, and going on to an intrinsic structure (atoms, elementary particles, and so forth) which determines the overall order of the movement; that is, how different movements in different places and times are related.

We may now add a more modern insight (which Leonardo probably understood implicitly):

3    A deeper and more extensive inner movement creates, maintains, and ultimately dissolves structure.

For example, the inner movements of electrons, protons, and neutrons will, under certain conditions, create and maintain the structure of a fluid, while under different conditions they will dissolve this structure.

However, the analysis in terms of separate and relatively fixed sorts of separate entities, such as particles of fluid, atoms, electrons, protons, or neutrons, is only a descriptive convenience, and does not correspond to the actual nature of "what is." Indeed, each entity is only *relatively* stable. For example, if the fluid is placed under a fire it dissolves into a moving flow of gas. Similarly, at higher temperatures (in the sun, or in an atomic explosion) the atoms out of which the gas is constituted break down and dissolve into more subtle forms of movement (such as neutrinos and radiant energy).

*There is nothing known that does not ultimately dissolve into movement in this way.* As with the vortices, we may find it convenient to describe the movement as if it were carried out by a set of stable and separately existent entities. But, more deeply, all has to be understood directly as relationship in undivided movement of the whole. In this movement, there is NO THING. Rather, "things" are abstracted out of the movement in our perception and thought, and any such abstraction fits the real movement only up to a point, and within limits. Some "things" may last for a very long time and be fairly stable, while others are as ephemeral as the shapes abstracted in perceptions of clouds.

It is important to emphasize that movement means not just the motion of an object through space, but also much more subtle orders of change, development, and evolution of every kind. For example, consider the movement of a symphony. This is expressed in terms of notes, which are sound waves (vibratory motions of molecules of air). But the essence of the movement cannot be understood in terms of such ideas of the motions of objects through space. This is made very clear if one considers how inappropriate it would be to talk about the "motion of a symphony" (at most this might perhaps refer to the displacement of the orchestra through space on a train). It would also evidently be inappropriate to talk about the *process* of a symphony. Indeed, the word "process" is based on the verb "to proceed," which means "to step forward." It thus refers to a particular kind of movement which goes step by step, with one step following another. However, the movement of a symphony involves a total ordering that is not essentially related to a process of time (though a process of time is involved in playing the notes, in a proper order). Indeed, one may in principle apprehend the whole movement of a symphony at any moment.

It is clear then that in an art form such as music one can have a direct sense of what it means for there to be a movement without some definite thing that is "doing the moving." Indeed, such movement is ultimately apprehended in a yet more subtle *movement of attention*, which is involved in all our sensory perceptions, and in the act of understanding the whole of perception and thought. And if we come to consider a living being, this attention is drawn to yet another form of movement, in which all the various functions are organized to work together to create and maintain the whole organism.

It is perhaps helpful here to note that the root of the word "organize" is related to the Greek "ergon," which is based on a verb meaning "to work," and that this verb is also the root of the word "energy," which thus means literally "to work within." If we think of the movement of life as an "organizing energy" that is "working within" the movements in the organs, in the cells, and, indeed, even in the atoms and elementary particles and thus ultimately merging with the universal field movement, this would perhaps help further in giving a feeling for what it means to take movement as primary.

The activity of this organizing energy is then what leads to the growth and sustenance of life in each organism, and to the evolution of ever-new forms of organism. When an organism dies, the movement of its "organizing energy" ceases, so that it dissolves ultimately into inorganic ("unorganized") matter. In earlier times, the prevailing world view was that there is a spiritual substance (a soul) which "does the organizing" and which departs when the organism dies. But now we can take it that the essence of life *is* the movement of organizing energy, and we do not think of a special "soul substance" that would produce or carry this energy.

By considering the primary significance of movement in this general sense, which includes art, inward experience at the psychological level, and what is to be meant by life, we can perhaps indicate at least the germ of a different world view, which can function to call attention to our outward perceptions and inward feelings in a new way, so that we can be free of the habitual and automatic function of the traditional view that this movement is meaningless, without some thing that is "doing the moving."

## On art, science, mathematics, and their general significance for "the good"

It is important to consider more carefully the difference between the approach of the scientist and that of the artist to the question of the nature of movement which has been discussed above. This is an example of the separation that has grown up between art and science. Actually, in early times man's activities were an undivided whole, in which science and art were not separate. Similarly, young children do not tend, of their own accord, to separate such activities. What happens is that they are gradually trained to think, feel, perceive, and act in terms of this kind of separation (as happened to mankind in general with the growth of civilization). Thus, what is natural and spontaneous to man is the wholeness of art and science, and the present approach that is common in society is a form of fragmentation that has been brought about by a process of conditioning.

A further fragmentation has arisen within science, which has split into science proper and mathematics. Thus there are now three separate fields: art, science, and mathematics. If we keep in mind that in origin all three spring from the one undivided human impulse, we can see that some understanding of their deep relationship may be obtained by considering how people thought about them long ago when there was less tendency to separate these fields.

If one looks into this, one finds that the consideration of early derivations of words helps to provide such an understanding in a surprisingly large number of cases. Of course, one has to be careful because many word usages develop accidentally. Nevertheless, with most key abstract words, one does indeed find that early meanings do call attention to a generally relevant kind of overall significance that tends to be lost in modern fragmentary ways of using such words.

A very good case in point is provided by considering the word "art." The original meaning of this word is "to fit." This meaning survives in articulate, article, artisan, artifact, and so on. Of course, in modern times the word "art" has come to mean mainly "to fit, in an aesthetic and emotional sense." However, the other words listed above show that art can also call attention to fitting in a functional sense. The fact that we are hardly aware of the syllable "art" in words such as articulate or artifact is an indication of an implicit but very deeply penetrating fragmentation in our thought between the aesthetic, emotional aspects of life and its practical functional aspects. This fragmentation tends to operate also in the meaning of the word "beauty," which is, according to the dictionary, "to fit in every sense." Nevertheless, this word also tends mainly to emphasize aesthetic and emotional fitting, even though, of course, it is sometimes applied to function, as in the sentence "This machine runs beautifully."

Let us then go on to consider the early meaning of the word "science," which is "to know." This evidently includes the knowledge of useful function but goes on to a knowledge that provides general theoretical insight, and even an overall world view, in the manner discussed earlier. Such knowledge is tested by seeing whether it fits broader aspects of the reality in which we live, in the first instance with the aid of observing instruments, and eventually by seeing how it is functionally fitted to useful purposes. The fitting of knowledge to useful function is what is emphasized in *technology* (from the Greek "techne," meaning "the work of an artisan").

Ultimately, the movement of knowing goes on to reach the level of philosophy, which is literally "love of wisdom." By now, philosophy has become one fragmentary field of specialization among many, but originally it meant a wholeness of understanding whose end was a kind of skill in seeing all knowledge as "fitting together." Thus, in its deepest and most comprehensive meaning, to know is an art, the impulse from which springs "love of wisdom."

The original source of the word "mathematics" is a Greek verb meaning "to understand" or "to learn." Mathematics is also, in essence, an art, but its aim is to make structures of thought which fit rationally and which are thus suitable for understanding and for learning. The "medium" of mathematical art is thus abstract symbolic thought, whereas what is usually called art works with a sensually perceptible medium. This is how the two kinds of art differ. But the creative mathematician is like any other creative artist in that he has to see new orders and structures which are embodied in some way in the medium in which he works. (He can also, of course, function as an artisan when he applies the results of such creation to useful ends.)

It can be seen that, in a very profound sense, all these activities are concerned with fitting, i.e. with art. All that man does is a kind of art, and this implies skill in doing things, as well as perception of how things fit or do not fit. This is indeed self-evident for the visual or musical artist as well as for the artisan. It is true also for the scientist and the mathematician, but less evident. It is therefore worthwhile to go in more detail here into the notion of science and mathematics as forms of art.

Finally, let us consider the act of *reasoning*, which is of primary significance in science and mathematics. Now, the word "reason" comes from the Latin "ratio." But, of course, this is more general in meaning than mere numerical proportions. Rather, qualitative similarity in relationships is included as well.

Here we may consider again—as discussed in the previous essay—Newton's insight into the law of gravity: "As the apple falls, so does the moon, and so indeed does all matter." Newton saw this in a flash of overall perception or understanding of an essentially poetic nature. But we can put what he saw into a more "prosaic" form as:

$$A : B :: C : D :: E : F$$

This means that the successive positions, A and B, of the apple are related to each other, as are successive positions C and D of the moon and as are the successive positions E and F of any moving body. Thus, we have a statement expressing a universal fitting of ratio or reason.

Since this statement applies to *all*, it follows that the ratio in question is *necessary*, meaning it cannot be otherwise. And thus, we have a *law* of nature which is a statement of inner or rational necessity. This is to be distinguished from external necessity, which is merely experienced outwardly as a fact, but which is not understood in its inner meaning. For example, it can be said that it is a hard necessity, imposed from outside, that a man caught in a desert without food or water must die. But when men rationally understand the inner necessities of the laws of growth of plants and of the flow of water, then the desert can be transformed so that the hardness of external necessity "melts" into the limitless possibilities revealed by insight into rational necessity.

In essence, rational necessity has to be apprehended in a kind of act of perception or insight similar to that in which Newton saw the universal law of motion of matter. From such a perception, more systematic theoretical structures of language and thought are created, used, and tested, in a kind of work that can, in some ways, be compared with that of the artisan. Ultimately, these theories lead to an overall world view such as that to which classical physics gave rise; and when any particular theoretical notions and world views persistently fail to fit new observation, they are dropped to leave room for new creative insights that can give rise to further new theories and world views. So, one can say that theories and world views arise and follow each other in a way that can be properly understood by regarding them as art forms.

In such a development, the main function of mathematics is then to create structures of thought and language appropriate for calling attention to rational necessity in an orderly way, which are highly articulated, and follow fairly well-defined logical rules. As in science, the essence of the art is in flashes of creative insight into new forms of universal ratio. Ultimately, logical rules are developed in the skillful fitting of such perceptions of universal ratio to particular cases in a kind of work that can be compared with that of the artisan. Thus, the following of logical rules is an important aspect of the function of universal ratio or reason, but not its primary impulse from which the art of mathematics springs. Indeed, it is not even the main distinguishing characteristic of good mathematics (as can be seen from the fact that an argument can be formally logical but irrational, while it can be formally in contradiction, and yet rational in its deeper or implicit meaning).

It has to be emphasized that universal ratio is not merely or even mainly a statement of what is common to all, that is, of general similarity. Rather, it is an ordered structure of differences or divisions, which are all related, and whose relationships are seen as *forming* the particular or the individual.

One can usefully indicate what is meant here with the aid of a work of art [see Figure 4.1]. In this design, which is based on a Moorish arabesque, one can see many orders emerging in the form of lines that extend across the whole pattern. These orders may be considered to play the role of the universal. Particular geometrical objects, such as triangles, quadrilaterals, and hexagons, are then formed or created in the intersection of the universal orders. Thus, it is evident that the universal is not to be regarded as just a set of properties (e.g. shape) that is common to all the particular geometrical objects.

When looked at in this way, the relationship in the design can help call attention to the true meaning of universal ratio or reason: that in the act of rational understanding the individual is raised to the level of the universal, by being perceived as a particular creation of the latter, rather than as a separately existent thing or object. (But, as was pointed out earlier, it has to be kept in mind that any given expression of the universal will fit only within certain limits and that, beyond these limits, a new expression of the universal will be needed.)

This overall notion of what is to be meant by universal ratio or reason evidently fits the world view discussed earlier in which a primary role is given to undivided wholeness in movement. It implies, of course, that a new kind of mathematics has to be developed to fit in with this new world view. Thus, current mathematics is based largely on set theory, which is in turn an articulation of the traditional world view in which the whole of existence is regarded as constituted out of collections of separately existent things. What is now needed is a mathematics in which the primary function of symbols is to call attention directly to aspects of a whole movement, and to call attention to particular things, or sets of things, only in some secondary function, which abstracts such things as relatively invariant features of the movement. (Some preliminary work along these lines of a mathematical and scientific nature has been done by the author, which will be published later.)[1]

It is clear, then, that reasoning is to be regarded as an art. And thus, in a deep sense, the artist, the scientist, and the mathemati-

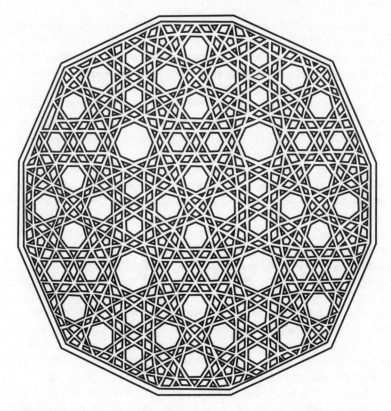

*Figure 4.1* Emergent universal orders
Reproduced with the kind permission of the artist, Ensor Holiday, from the Altair Collection.

cian are concerned with art in its most general significance, that is, with *fitting*.

Of course, there are important differences in the work of the artist, the scientist, and the mathematician. As pointed out earlier, the artist works in some sensually perceptible medium, to create structures that "fit," while the medium of such creation for the mathematician and the scientist is primarily abstract thought. However, whereas the creative action of the mathematician generally remains within the field of abstract thought, the work of the scientist requires that, in the long run, there be a fit not only rationally within such thought considered by itself, but also between this thought and broader aspects of the reality in which we live. To this end, the scientist creates new instruments designed to help to put his ideas to more precise, detailed, and sensitive tests than is possible without the use of such instruments. In doing this, he develops a certain skill (resembling that of the artisan) in being able to see how his ideas may be related to the functioning of his instruments in experiments. All of this may be called the "art form" of science, which evidently differs from that of the visual or musical art and that of mathematics in that in these latter the main emphasis is on a certain kind of "internal fitting" in the work itself.

However, what is of primary significance in the present context is not a consideration of such differences in "art forms" of the creative work carried out by different groups of people. Rather, it is that each human being *is* artist, scientist, and mathematician all in one, in the sense that he is most profoundly concerned with aesthetic and emotional fitting, with functional and practical fitting, with universal rational fitting, and, more generally, with fitting between his world view and his overall experience with the reality in which he lives. Even in his particular work he is always concerned with all these kinds of fitting, though, of course, with different sorts of emphasis. So one has to begin with a general feeling for the whole of human activity, both in society and in the individual. This is to be described as art: the action of fitting.

One may ask: "What does it mean to fit?" Evidently, this cannot possibly be given a complete analysis or explanation. Indeed, even if we thought we had one, we would have to ask: "Does it fit the real nature of fitting?" Thus, we would be thrown back to an act of perception, feeling, and skilled response to what is actually going on in life as a whole. For example, we would not attempt to define what sort of fitting makes a great work of art. Why, then, should we ask for a similar definition in connection with life as a whole, the understanding of which requires an art of a yet higher order?

In this art of life as a whole we have to be both creative artists and skilled artisans. We are thus always in the act of fitting an ever-changing reality so that there is no fixed or final goal to be attained. Rather, at each moment the end and the means are both to be described as the action of making every aspect fit.

This notion of fitting extends into all aspects of life, including even those that have been called "moral" or "ethical" and which have to do with "the good." The word "good" is indeed derived from an Anglo-Saxon root (the same as that of "gather" and "together") which means "to join." And so it may be suggested that early notions of "the good" implied some kind of "fitting together" in all that man does. The fact that the Latin word "bene," meaning "good," and the word "bellus," meaning "beauty," are related in origin further confirms the suggestion that this is generally how people may have looked on such questions. Recalling that beauty means "to fit in every respect," we could say that such a significance of "the good" is still relevant today. In other words, the good is that which fits, not only in practical function and in our feelings and aesthetic sensibilities, but also that which, by its action, leads to an ever-wider and deeper sort of fitting, in every phase of life, both for the individual and for society as a whole.

As Socrates pointed out, all men desire the good. Indeed, how could a man possibly desire that which he *sees* as not properly fitting, in contexts which he feels to be important? Even a man who is self-centered, ruthless, and ambitious will, for example, generally be found to look on what he is trying to do as good.

The difficulty is, of course, that men have confused and fragmentary notions as to what *is* the good. Such fragmentary notions of the good will inevitably divide men, both in themselves and from each other, and so must lead to unending conflict. Thus, what is at the origin of evil is just the fact that each man pursues his own fragmentary notion of the good.

To end this fragmentation is clearly of crucial importance if man is to cease to accomplish evil in the very act in which he pursues the good. So, what is needed is to pause and to inquire into the origin of this fragmentation in a mode of thought in which the separation of art, science, and mathematics from each other and from questions of morals and ethics plays a key role.

It is widely believed, for example, that in some sense, art, science, and mathematics are "morally neutral." Thus, it is said that scientific knowledge may be used either for good or for evil ends, according to the decisions of those who control public affairs, while artistic skills can similarly be used either for true cultural enlightenment or for making propaganda that twists men's minds in destructive ways. But such a separation between the content of men's work and its ultimate human significance is itself a result of the overall condition of fragmentation that has largely prevailed throughout the ages. Indeed, if men were generally considering knowledge as an unbroken whole (as is implied, for example, in the original meaning of philosophy as "love of wisdom") they would understand that this whole has to fit in every aspect of life. So it would be clear that there is no meaning to such a notion of overall fitting if its end is not "the good." To give primary emphasis to the question of whether or not science and art, in their present fragmented states, are "morally neutral" is evidently, then, to take attention away from the key point. This is that each individual has in his own mind to see the need to be an unbroken whole, and not a being who is separated, for example, into technological, sociological, and psychological fragments.

To expect that men will cease to engage in this sort of fragmentation through moral exhortation, through compulsion, through being convinced of what is right, or through a new organization of society is to try to solve the problem of fragmentation by engaging in more of the fragmentary mode of thought that produces the problem. Rather, what we have to do is to give serious and sustained attention to this mode of thought itself. And this is what we are beginning to do when we see how we have been conditioned to split art, science, mathematics, and the desire for "the good" into separate compartments of life, so that we are not able to see the oneness of the deep impulse toward "fitting" that is behind all of these.

## On metaphysics and the movement of universal fitting

If, as was suggested in the previous section, the essence of human life is art—a whole movement in which end and means are the action of fitting—it is clearly of key importance to give attention to the fitting or non-fitting of our overall world views in the broader reality within which we live. For a world view is concerned not merely with particular details or aspects, but rather with *all*, including external nature, ourselves, and how we are related to external nature and to each other. So, if our world views do not fit, this will give rise to a very far-reaching and deep confusion that penetrates into every aspect of life (even into that which is meant by "the good," toward which all men cannot do other than strive).

Generally speaking, our world views start out in a highly implicit and tacit form which operates largely "subliminally," in a way of which we are hardly aware. The possibility of giving attention to the question of whether such world views fit or not depends, to a considerable extent, on our ability to express them explicitly. Indeed, mankind has, from early times, generally tried to do this, in a form that has come to be called *metaphysics*.

Metaphysics is in essence a systematic way of attempting to say something relevant about *all*. For example, in ancient Greece philosophers considered a series of notions such as "*all* is flux," "*all* is fire," "*all* is water," "*all* is air," and so on. Following along in this series, Democritus said that "*all* is atoms," moving in a void, and this was later developed to lay the foundation for the current scientific tradition, in which *all* is regarded as a set of "basic building blocks," such as elementary particles following well-defined and known (or knowable) laws in their motions through the void.

It can thus be seen that metaphysics has the general form "*all* is $X$." In the current scientific tradition, $X$ is generally taken to be a set of basic elements which are regarded as "universal building blocks." But in the present essay we have begun to explore the notion that $X$ is an unbroken and undivided movement in which apparently separate and distinct things are abstracted only as relatively stable aspects.

As has been indicated above, however, metaphysics is relevant not only to nature but also to human beings, both individually and socially. And so, we have indeed inquired into the metaphysical notion that *all* human life is art. If we stopped here and did not extend this inquiry to the whole of nature as well, this would, however, divide existence into two parts, the activity of one of which, i.e. mankind, would be described as "art," while that of the other part—nature—would be described as "something other than art." So we would have come to a metaphysics in which *all* was separated into two disjoint fragments, man and nature. But this would, of course, contradict our primary metaphysical statement that *all* is an unbroken and undivided movement in which apparently separate things are abstracted as relatively stable aspects.

We are thus led to explore the notion that, in some sense, the action of nature as well as that of mankind may be regarded as art, i.e. fitting together. As a first step in such an exploration we may consider the fact that in earlier days man did not generally feel himself to be as sharply separated from nature as he now tends to do. So he probably would have found no great difficulty in thinking that the primary movement in nature was to be understood in terms of notions such as "fitting" and "not fitting." (Indeed, many earlier forms of metaphysics did look at nature in some such way.)

However, since then we have been conditioned to think in terms of the atomistic or "building block" metaphysics which tends to lead us to look at what is going on in nature as a mechanical movement of parts without any overall organizational function. Thus, the original atomic theory of Democritus took the atoms to be separate beings moving in "the void" and therefore without contact. Any organized arrangement of atoms would then have to be due to chance. Later it was proposed that atoms have forces of attraction and repulsion between them, so that stable arrangements are not due purely to chance. Nevertheless, in an ultimate analysis, any organized function is still explained as the result of the mechanical interplay of forces and motions which is dependent on conditions that are, at bottom, of a fortuitous nature.

This view is carried into modern biology, in which it is supposed that life emerged in this mechanical interplay and that the evolution of organisms is due to fortuitous changes or mutations in the structure of DNA molecules. The question of whether any such mutation will survive depends on how the resulting organism *adapts* to its environment. Of course, "to adapt" means in essence the same as "to fit." So, in some very implicit sense, a kind of notion of "art" has been brought into the basic theories of biology. But this notion has only a secondary kind of significance, in the sense that any such fitting has to be explained ultimately in terms of the mechanical interplay of forces and motions in the basic atomic structure of matter.

This prevailing metaphysical view may be summed up in the statement that *all* fitting (or organization) is ultimately either the result of chance coincidences in the mechanical motions of a set of universal building blocks, or else the result of purposeful human activity. It follows, then, that "non-fitting" is what is natural and given, while wherever "fitting" is encountered it requires a special explanation along the lines indicated above.

What we are doing in this essay is to consider what it means to turn this prevailing metaphysics of science "upside down" by exploring the notion that a kind of art—a movement of fitting together—is what is universal, both in nature and in human activities. Apparent non-fitting is then what will be given special explanation, as a kind of limited autonomy of relatively stable forms that can be abstracted from the whole movement.

If we note that human activities are described by the word "artifact," which means literally "that which has been made to fit," we can see the need, in our new world view, for a related word to call attention to how fitting takes place more generally. We thus introduce a new word—*artamovement*, which means "the movement of fitting." And so the metaphysics that we are now exploring can be expressed as "*all* is artamovement." Not only is inanimate nature created and formed in art movement, but so also is life, in all its evolving and developing forms, going on to man, with his capacity for perception, feeling, thought, and action. It follows then, of course, that the creation of artifacts by human beings is now to be regarded as a special case of *artamovement*.

As an example of this way of developing a general world view, we can consider Einstein's notion (discussed in an earlier section) of whole movement in a universal field, along with its law, which is an expression of universal ratio or reason in all aspects of movement. We then find that, as Einstein suggested, such a law allows for the abstraction of particle-like forms (intense but narrowly localized regions of the field) having a certain relative and limited sort of autonomy and stability.

We see in this way how a law of fitting of the whole is able to explain what has, in earlier forms of metaphysics, been regarded as a kind of independence of separate parts. Thus, if we ignored the whole field movement from which the particle-like forms are abstracted, we might then imagine that the various "particles" are separately existent entities that move mechanically, in a way that has no natural tendency to fit together. By ceasing to be aware of this act of abstraction, we might further conclude that everything, including life and intelligent perception, is ultimately to be understood as nothing but a fortuitous result of such mechanical movements. Clearly, however, this is an excessive simplification. For the law of the whole movement not only is such as to allow for the abstraction of particles with a certain kind of relative autonomy, but also implies that this autonomy is limited and that, in new contexts, such "particles" may work together in a more organized sort of movement, the laws of which are not completely expressible in terms of those of the particle-like abstractions alone. So we do not have to suppose that life and intelligent perception can be explained completely through the properties of particle-like abstractions (though, of course, we admit that such explanations may fit, up to a point and within certain limits).

It has to be kept in mind, in any case, that all that is known about the world through scientific research, and indeed in any other way, depends ultimately on living human beings who are capable of intelligent perception. In this perception, a certain aesthetic and emotional response is of crucial importance for indicating whether what we see makes sense or not (we first become aware of contradiction as an unspecifiable feeling, that something is wrong somewhere, and then we may have a vague intimation or "hunch" as to what is wrong and what to do about it). It is thus arbitrary to separate the intellectual aspect of the movement (insight into universal ratio or reason) from its emotional, aesthetic aspects and from its aspect as ordinary sense perception. Any one of these aspects may be emphasized in a particular case, but, in general, all of them have to be seen as a single whole.

There is indeed no good reason for the traditional view, in which this whole is fragmented into two disjoint parts—one of which is taken to be the rational fitting of function, considered to be public, impersonal, and objective, while the other of which is taken to be the response through aesthetic sensibilities and feelings, considered to be private, personal, and a matter of purely subjective tastes and preferences. Rather, neither of these aspects is ultimately purely objective or purely subjective.

Indeed, even what have generally been regarded as objectively valued laws of physics (e.g. those of elementary particles) are found to fit in only limited contexts, and these limits are in some sense an expression of our own particular conditioning to certain habits of thinking, feeling, and observing which suit the sorts of tastes and preferences generally developed in our society, with its special historical background. On the other hand, as has been suggested here, universally significant aspects of "the law of the whole movement" which have been missed in such physical laws may be revealed in the organization of function of living beings (such as ourselves), and in their overall response to the natural environment, which includes not only sense perception and the apprehension of its meaning through universal ratio or reason, but also aesthetic sensibilities and feelings which play an equally important role in this response.

To see the world in this way as a totality of movement, sensed and felt on one side as beauty, and apprehended on another side as function ordered by rational law, requires an unrestricted attention to fitting and non-fitting in all its aspects. Evidently, this will not be possible if we go on with the commonly accepted separation between aesthetic-emotional and rational-functional aspects of perception.

So we see in yet another way that the wholeness of existence can be understood properly only when we ourselves are whole and free of the prevailing fragmentation to which we have been conditioned.

## On truth, metaphysics, and language

We have come, in a manner indicated in the previous section, to inquire into a new form of metaphysics, in which all is taken to be *artamovement*: a universal movement of fitting. In such an inquiry, how will it be possible for us to know whether what we think and say is true or not? Indeed, what does it mean, in connection with metaphysical notions, even to raise the question of truth or falsity?

When one discusses what is to be meant by truth in such a broad context, however, one is raising issues of great subtlety that are very far-reaching and deep in their ultimate implications. We shall see, in fact, that the consideration of these issues leads to an examination not only of the proper function of metaphysical thought, but also of our general notions concerning ourselves and the world in which we live, and ultimately of the language which we use in talking about these very issues.

In going into these questions we shall begin by discussing the simple context of truth of statements and then go on from there to consider what is to be meant by truth in its wider significance. If, for example, one says "There is a pencil on the table," one can see that what this statement means fits what is actually observed. On the other hand, if one says "There is a cat on this table," one can see that what the statement means does not fit what is actually observed. So the essential point to be noted here is that the truth or falsity of a statement is apprehended in an act of perception, in which what is to be seen is not mainly what appears in the observed fact nor even in the meanings evoked by our statements but, rather, *whether these two fit each other or not*.

A rather commonly accepted theory of how meaning and observed fact are related is that a true statement expresses a *correspondence* between idea and fact. In one form of this theory it is said that an idea evoked by a true statement is in a kind of *image* correspondence with the fact (that is, it resembles what is to be observed in *function* so that it corresponds not only to the fact as it is but also to potentialities and possibilities for changing the fact).

Of course, such modes of correspondence are a *kind* of fitting and can therefore describe certain limited aspects of what is to be meant by fitting truth. For example, we can correctly *imagine* (make a mental image of) an object which is not present in perception, and by further supposing this object to obey certain laws of nature we can make this mental image into a sort of model. But the general nature of fitting goes immensely beyond that of mere correspondence. Thus, the function of the brain and that of the liver fit each other in the overall organization of the body and yet these are neither images nor models of each other. What is being suggested here is that the general relationship of true notions and observed facts is a sort of organic fitting of functions in the whole movement of perception, thought, and communication, rather than a form of correspondence. As pointed out in earlier sections, we are emphasizing here that thought is to be treated in every way as a real function that "works together" with other functions within a large totality of overall organization of human activity in general.

In this totality one of the main functions of a statement is to communicate an *ordering of attention*, which is thus directed momentarily to some aspect of the total field of observation. For example, attention may be ordered so as to focus on what is actually meant in a statement by means of the action of *pointing*. (Indeed, the word "index," as applied to a finger, is a form of the verb "to indicate.") Or else, this meaning may be indicated by some order of description appearing in the statement itself. The simplest form of such descriptive indication is to use an order of correspondence. Thus, to say "Look for a row of trees" means to direct one's attention to a possible correspondence between the order in the general notion of "a row" and a similar order of "actual trees" that is to be observed. But, more generally, there is no such simple correspondence. For example, in a mathematical discussion one may say "Look for the contradiction in this argument." Evidently, one does not begin with some sort of image or model of contradiction and then direct one's attention to a possible correspondence between this image or model and what one actually perceives in the argument. Rather, to look for a contradiction is like looking for features that do not fit in "a whole picture."

As pointed out in the previous section, at this very deep level to see what fits or does not fit involves, in the first instance, an unspecifiable feeling that "something is wrong somewhere." From such feelings and aesthetic sensibilities a more precise notion of just what it is that may be "wrong" tends gradually to arise. So, in this context, to perceive what is indicated is evidently an *art*, requiring a kind of skill that cannot be reduced to a method of comparison between "what one actually sees" and some well-defined "image" or "model."

It is clear, then, that, generally speaking, the perception of whether a particular statement fits or does not fit what is actually to be observed involves a movement of attention of a very high order of subtlety, which can easily fail to be taken into account at the level of language and abstract thought. Indeed, as pointed out earlier in this essay, such movement of attention is an aspect of the *symbolic function of language*. This function is carried out in a very fast and complex overall response involving imagery, ideas, urges, motivations, and reflexes to action, which is evidently enormously beyond the possibility of being given a detailed description or analysis. Similarly, what it means to say that the complex of movement "fits" or "does not fit" those aspects of the field of observation to which it calls attention also cannot possibly be specified in detail, since the movements involved in sense perception are perhaps even more subtle than those involved in the symbolic function. Nevertheless, our ability to apprehend the truth and falsity of statements clearly depends on a capacity to see such fitting or non-fitting in a "split second." This sort of apprehension takes place not only in sense perception and in perception of the content of our thought but also when observation is focused on the mode of functioning of such thoughts. For example, the statement "My present mode of thinking is disordered and inattentive" gives rise to a very subtle and complex symbolic function which orders attention toward the observation of inner movements and sensations that may be able to reveal the truth or falsity of this sort of statement.

To sum up, then, what is presupposed in discussing the truth or falsity of a statement is that, in some way, the symbolic function of such a statement orders attention to indicate or point to a related (but not necessarily corresponding) order that is to be observed, and that there is a yet higher and more subtle movement of perception in which it can be seen whether the order to which attention has been called fits or does not fit that which is to be observed.

As long as the symbolic function of a statement contains some sort of indication "pointing to" a perceivable context in which it may be seen either to fit or not to fit, then the question of what is to be meant by its truth or falsity is thus fairly clear. But as our thought goes on to ever more abstract levels, the indication of such a context tends to grow more and more ambiguous. When we come to the general metaphysical statement "*all* is *X*," this ambiguity is so great that the function of "pointing" has broken down altogether. Of course, with a concrete and specified totality (for example, *all* the books on a given shelf) this difficulty with the meaning of "all" does not arise. But how is it possible to order attention to look at an unspecified and unlimited "all" so as to see whether the symbolic function of a proposed idea fits or does not fit *this* "all"?

In what way, then, are we to understand the proper symbolic function of a metaphysical statement? Perhaps some insight into this question can be obtained by adding to the metaphysical form "*all* is *X*," a further form introduced by Korzybski: "Whatever we say 'all' is, it isn't." Not only is "all" more than anything that can be contained in our knowledge; it is also different, in the sense that our knowledge is not an absolute truth and so becomes false when extrapolated without limit. Indeed, as pointed out in earlier sections, reality as a whole is vast and immense, so that anything that is known ultimately merges and shades into a measureless unknown in which the totality of what mankind may know, at any particular stage, has its origin, its sustenance, and its ultimate dissolution.

But, evidently, even Korzybski's statement itself suffers from the defect which it was designed to point out. For it, too, is a statement about "all," and thus, through its own meaning, it collapses into a contradiction. What this signifies is that the whole attitude that leads one to attempt to say something *true* about "all" is what has to be dropped. Rather, as pointed out earlier, metaphysics is an explicit expression of a world view. It is thus to be regarded as an art form, resembling poetry in some ways and mathematics in others, rather than as an attempt to say something true about reality as a whole.

As was pointed out in earlier sections with regard to our world views, the function of metaphysics is to help in the overall organization of our knowledge and experience. And, thus, the notion that metaphysics aims at *truth of content* is seen to interfere with its proper function. Indeed, to assume that the content of the statement "all is $X$" is true leads to the conclusion that it is *always* true and so implies the logical impossibility of any change in the metaphysics that may be needed to fit new observation and experience, going beyond the limits of adequacy of fit of older world views. However, if we understand that any given metaphysics is in only a particular art form, then we see that we are free to drop it when it persistently fails to fit observation and experience. And so metaphysics will become a means of bringing about creative change and development in our overall thought, rather than (as it has generally been thus far) a means of blocking such change.

The truth of metaphysics is, then, not to be understood as being in any particular content that it may have at a given stage but, rather, in a right overall function which is continually allowing attention to go to the question of how any particular metaphysics fits, or fails to fit, our overall knowledge and experience as this develops and changes.

The need in this way to consider both truth of content and *truth in function* is, however, already implicit in the common usage of language. Thus, the Latin word for true, "verus" (e.g. as exemplified in the English "veracity"), goes back to an ancient Indo-European root meaning "that which is" (which carries forward to the modern English "were" and the German "wahr"). On the other hand, the English "true" goes back to an Anglo-Saxon root, meaning "honest" or "faithful." In the first of these usages truth of content (that is, fitting of ideas to "what is") is emphasized, while in the second what is emphasized is truth in action and in function (that the whole mode of function of the mind fits what is needed properly to perceive the relationship between content and "what is"). Evidently, without honesty in function, truth of content has little meaning (individuals with dishonest aims can twist statements with a true content to lead to false implications and meanings, in the form of "half-truths"). So we may say that what is needed in metaphysics is *truth in function:* a function that is not dominated by the search for a feeling of security and that therefore does not hold to a fixed content when there are indications that this content no longer fits new experience.

Such built-in function is, however, impeded and often even

blocked by the prevailing metaphysical notion that everything is analyzable into a set of basic elements (such as particles). As pointed out earlier, it is not mainly the particular content of this notion that interferes with truth in function. Rather, it is the generally prevailing attitude of regarding such a notion as an absolute and therefore unalterable truth that gets in the way of the proper function of metaphysical thought.

This sort of attitude to the metaphysics of analysis into parts has its roots, however, in a context going far beyond that of scientific research alone. Indeed, it is to be found in almost every phase of life, as a tacit world view, in a form generally taken to be "common sense," or "intuitive obvious truths," or "the way everything is." Thus, from early childhood we learn to accept the notion that the world is constituted out of a tremendous number of different and separately existent things. Some of these things are inanimate objects, some are alive, some are human beings. And to each person there is a certain very special one of these things, which is *himself*. This "self" is viewed, in the first instance, as a physical body, sharply bounded by the surface of the skin, and then as a "mental entity" (also called the psyche or "the soul") which is "within" this physical body and which is taken to be the very essence of the individual human being. The notion of a separately existent "self" thus follows as an aspect of the generally accepted metaphysics, which implies that *everything* is of this nature.

It has to be emphasized that this generally accepted metaphysics is not commonly known in the form of an explicit statement as given above. Rather, it is built up, mainly tacitly, in countless conclusions from experience over a lifetime. Because this accumulated residue of tacit metaphysical thought is largely automatic and habitual, we are not aware of it *as such*. And so, as pointed out in an earlier section, we do not see the one undivided movement in which the thought actually *functions* to give shape to outward perception and to inward feelings, motivations, urges, and so forth. As a result, the effects of this metaphysical thought on perception and feeling are experienced as a reality that seems to arise independently of such thought and that apparently encompasses both the "external world" of man and society and the "internal world" of the "self." Similarly, the content of the metaphysics is experienced as a set of "self-evident truths" or "eternal verities that mankind has always known." So, a complex and very pervasive illusion is created, in which the divisions in the content of thought are projected into the experiencing of what is sensed as real and into the very act of perception, of truth, itself. In this way, one becomes almost incapable of being aware of the falsity of this whole mode of functioning.

What is needed to see through the illusion is to perceive that the division of the whole of existence into separate parts is only a convenient form of "metaphysical art" that fits our general experience within certain limits, and not an expression of "how things really are." Indeed, it is quite evident that there can be no such sharp division between things in reality. Thus, because of its atomic structure no object can have a sharp boundary. Rather, there is always an interpenetration of different kinds of atoms when two substances are in contact. In any case, as seen earlier, the atoms are constituted of elementary particles which all ultimately merge and unite in the whole movement of the universal field. And, if we think about the human being, we can see, in addition to all these considerations, that food, water, air, and other things are continually exchanged between the body and its environment through the surfaces of various membranes. Through the senses and the nervous system, man is also in perceptual contact with his natural and social environment. In this regard, it is especially important to realize that each man's thought arises in a cyclical movement in which he is exposed to the thought of other people and responds with a generally similar but somewhat different thought of his own. So it can be seen that, ultimately, all that man is, both physically and mentally, arises in his overall contacts with the whole world in which he lives.

It is clear, then, that one cannot actually observe a "self" that can be sharply distinguished from the total environment. Rather, in every aspect of his being, the boundary of an individual man is to be compared with that of a city—in the sense that it can be at times a useful abstraction, but that it is not a description of a real break or division in "what is." And, ultimately, the same is true of the boundary of anything.

And thus one can see that the notion of identity of each thing is also only a convenient abstraction which is, as it were, a complement to the notion that different things can be abstracted as separately existent. The word "identity" comes from the roots "id" and "entity," which show its meaning: "the same being." Thus, one may think that, *in essence*, each thing remains "always the same as it was." This notion is especially common with regard to the "self," which is generally supposed to have a permanent identity. Indeed, so strong is the belief in this identity that when people feel that they are losing it or do not know what it is they may experience a sense of profound disturbance, which has been described in literature as a need to search for "one's lost identity."

It is clear, however, that if each "thing" has its origin, its sustenance, and its ultimate dissolution in a broader whole, extending ultimately to the universal field movement from which even the atomic particles are abstracted, then there can be no meaning to saying that this thing is "always the same." Rather, the notion of some permanent essence which would be its "identity" is, like that of a sharp boundary, only a simplifying abstraction which may fit within certain limits. That is to say, when one regards things as permanently separate in their existence it follows that each of them must be characterized by some permanent essence or essential features which determine "what it is" and "how it differs from other things." So to assign an identity to a thing, considered to be separately existent, makes sense only when we regard such a way of thinking as a form of metaphysical art, and not, for example, as an expression of a principle of identity that would be a true statement about "what is".

As an example, we may consider a vortex in a fluid. Actually, there *is* no such entity as a vortex. It is merely an abstraction which focuses attention on certain relatively constant and separable features of the unceasing movement and flow from which the vortex form has been abstracted. To say that one vortex is "separated" from another by the fluid "between" them is evidently a metaphoric way of talking (that is, an art form) that may give a certain limited insight into what is actually happening. Likewise, to say that the vortex remains in essence the same (and thus to try to assert that it has an "identity") is just another side of this mode of thought.

Of course, we generally find it difficult to look at things in this way. Rather, in common experience things do as a rule seem to exist separately, each with its own identity. This is particularly noticeable with regard to the "self," which we tend to feel really is an autonomously existent thing and not merely an abstracted pattern of movement resembling a vortex, as an art form, created in a particular kind of metaphysics.

However, as has been seen, the notion that the "self" is an

abstraction from a whole movement, which thus has only a certain relative similarity or constancy of form and pattern of behavior, is what fits the actual facts of the case when these are looked at carefully. The generally prevailing impression that the "self" actually has an identity can, in fact, be seen to arise in the automatic and habitual function of metaphysical thought. As pointed out earlier, this function is such as to project the content of the metaphysics into our overall experience as an illusion of perceived reality, actual feeling, and universal truth. In this projection, the abstract divisions of our metaphysical thought are seen as a break-up of the whole field of existence into separate fragments, while the union of what is inside the divisions is seen as a permanent and unchanging identification of the nature of each fragment.

Of course, both the divisive and the uniting function of abstract thought can be useful and necessary when the thought is seen *as such*. But when we fail to see this, the significance of our experience as a whole is perceived wrongly, and thought becomes a means of creating a structure of illusion that makes everything seem both divided and unchangeable in its essential nature.

What is needed is, then, *an attention that is not limited to the shapes determined by metaphysical thought*. Rather, one has to be sensitive to the eternally changing differences that are actually to be observed within each thing, and to the unceasing emergence of new similarities and relationships across the boundaries of the various things. Such attention discloses the *abstract character* of perception in terms of separate things, each with a fixed essential nature. When one sees this abstract character *as such* he is able to use this mode of thought within the limits in which it fits, without mistaking its general metaphysics for "an absolute truth about the whole of reality." And so the mind is free, at any moment, to give attention to new differences and new similarities, allowing for the perception of a new structure of "things."

## NOTE

1   See Bohm, D. and Hiley, B. J. (1993) *The Undivided Universe*. London: Routledge.

# 5

# ART, DIALOGUE, AND THE IMPLICATE ORDER

## David Bohm interviewed by Louwrien Wijers

Q   Dr. Bohm, as we move into the twenty-first century, where do you believe we stand in physics?

DAVID BOHM   There have been two great revolutions at the beginning of the twentieth century; the theory of relativity and quantum theory, which implied very great changes in our concepts of matter. Since then physics has been developed largely on the basis of these two theories. But there are certain limits which are emerging now. One limit would be at the very, very short distances, where it would seem that all the current theories might break down altogether, including relativity, quantum theory, and the gravity theory.

The other limit is in cosmology, where people are pursuing these theories to the presumed origin of the universe, the so-called Big Bang. There again, one would expect the current theories to break down. In this regard I think that physics is discovering many new kinds of particles over the last period and is making discoveries in cosmology which are moving in that direction. It is still in a great state of flux. Yet we have not yet understood the meaning of the previous revolutions. If we now move from one position we do not understand to another we will get more and more confused.

Q   How did you yourself evolve after working with Niels Bohr and Albert Einstein?

BOHM   I didn't actually work with Bohr, though I did have talks with him. I discussed a number of times with Einstein. Afterwards we corresponded.

First I just studied quantum mechanics and relativity, and in doing this I began by more or less accepting the ideas of Niels Bohr. Later I wrote a book called *Quantum Theory*, in which I was really quite strongly in favor of his ideas as I understood them. Well, I became somewhat dissatisfied towards the end of this period, around 1950 when I finished the book. I sent copies of the book to various physicists, including Pauli, Bohr, and Einstein. Pauli liked the book. Einstein liked the book, but when I discussed it with him he said he was still not satisfied. Both of us felt that the key question was: "What is the nature of reality?" But, you see, Bohr's view is based on epistemology, on saying that all we can discuss is our knowledge of reality. I felt dissatisfied with that.

Q   Did you consider yourself to be a kind of revolutionary at that time?

BOHM   Not really. Initially I followed Bohr's view, you know. I thought we would make progress within that view, mainly in the direction of very, very short distances, where there were serious problems. However, I later became dissatisfied with the general interpretation of the theory because it didn't give a clear concept of reality. It only discussed what could be observed and measured. If you say "Fine, that's what it is," then you would still raise the question: "What can we nevertheless say about the nature of reality?"

Q   What was reality for you, then?

BOHM   Well, reality would mean something that would have some existence independently of being known. It might be that we would know it, but it didn't require that we would know it in order to exist. Now, it was difficult to see how this could be sustained finally in Bohr's view. I proposed another model that had some interesting implications, but it was not received well. Essentially the leading physicists did not accept it. Later I came to the implicate order, which had a similar aim.

Q   Was it your belief that there were destructive powers in the then prevailing mechanistic views in science?

BOHM   I was certainly dissatisfied with mechanism. I felt that mechanism and reductionism were destructive, as you say, that they would lead to a narrowing down of human thought, to focusing on some small thing, making it very rigid. Trying to contain life and mind and society and everything within this mechanism I think would have a bad effect. I don't think Bohr was actually a mechanist, but I felt that if we did not have some view of reality, it was unclear what we were talking about at all. I felt also that Bohr's view could lead to a certain kind of dogmatism, in which all these questions were just simply dismissed as having no significance.

Q   Do you feel that the scientist, like the artist, needs some kind of stirring of the muse?

BOHM   Yes, I think many, indeed most, scientists would agree with that. At least those I know. Certainly this was a common belief when I was younger. I think the scientific and the artistic spirit have something in common. The scientist wants not only to learn about the facts, but to understand how they cohere, fit together, and make a whole. He even uses criteria such as beauty and symmetry to help decide which theory he wants.

The scientist cannot capture the whole cosmos in thought. In his mind he makes a kind of microcosm, which we see as an analogue of the cosmos. In this way we try to get a feeling for the whole. The artist, I suppose, gets a feeling for the whole some other way.

Q   Is it true that the scientific spirit comes close to a kind of religious awareness?

BOHM   Yes, I would like to say that I read long ago, in some ancient saying, that there were three basic attitudes of spirit: the scientific, the artistic, and the religious. They have certain things in common and certain differences. I think this is essential.

One of the most essential points of the scientific spirit is to acknowledge the fact, or the interpretation of the fact, whether you like it or not. This means not to engage in wishful thinking, and not to reject something just because you don't like it. This is not a common attitude in life generally, and scientists have been at great pains in their struggle to establish this spirit. This is obviously necessary for the artist too since he cannot just simply depict things according to what pleases him, or in the way he would like them to be. The religious spirit requires the same thing, otherwise it will get lost in self-deception, as happens so easily.

Q   Can I take you back to your own theory which you describe as the implicate order? Where does it fit in?

BOHM    At that time I already had the notion that one needs to understand the reality of the process, and that quantum mechanics gave no picture, no notion of what was happening. It merely talked about the results of measurements and observations. From such results you can compute the probability of another observation, without any notion of how they are connected, except statistically.

Now, I tried to get some idea what might be the process implied by the mathematics of the quantum theory, and this process is what I called *enfoldment*. The mathematics itself suggests a movement in which everything, any particular element of space, may have a field which unfolds into the whole and the whole enfolds it in it. An example of that would be a hologram. In an ordinary photograph made by a lens you have a point-to-point correspondence. Each point in the object corresponds to a point in the image, more or less. Now, in a hologram the entire object is contained in each region of the hologram, enfolded as a pattern of waves, which can then be unfolded by shining light through it.

The suggestion is that if you look at the mathematics of the quantum theory it describes a movement of just this nature, a movement of waves that unfold and enfold throughout the whole of space. You could therefore say that everything is enfolded in this whole, or even in each part, and that it then unfolds. I call this an *implicate order*, the enfolded order, and this unfolds into an explicate order. The implicate is the enfolded order. It unfolds into the explicate order, in which everything is separated.

So I say that this movement is the basic movement suggested by the quantum theory. The best analogy to illustrate the implicate order is the hologram, as I said. I contrast this to a photograph. Every part of the hologram contains some information about the object, which is enfolded.

One may now notice that we don't need this hologram, because each part of space contains waves from everything, which enfold the whole room, the whole universe, the whole of everything. In the implicate order everything is thus internally related to everything, everything contains everything, and only in the explicate order are things separate and relatively independent.

Q    So you went far beyond the current theory.

BOHM   It did not change the mathematics of the theory. It was an interpretation to see what it means. You understand? Everybody has many experiences of this implicate order. The most obvious one is ordinary consciousness, in which consciousness enfolds everything that you know or see. It doesn't merely enfold the universe, but you act according to that content as well. Therefore you are internally related to the whole in the sense that you act according to the consciousness of the whole.

The enfolded order is a vast range of potentiality, which can be unfolded. The way it is unfolded depends on many factors. The way we think and so on is among those factors. The implicate order implies mutual participation of everything with everything. No thing is complete in itself, and its full being is realized only in that participation. The implicate order provides an image of how this participation might take place in physics in various ways.

In participation we bring out potentials which are incomplete in themselves, but it is only in the whole that the thing is complete. This makes it clear that we are not acting mechanistically, in the sense that we would be pushed and pulled by objects in the surroundings, but rather we act according to our consciousness of them, so if you are not conscious of them you cannot act intelligently towards them. Consciousness, therefore, is really our most immediate experience of this implicate order.

Ordinarily we aim for a literal picture of the world, but in fact we create a world according to our mode of participation, and we create ourselves accordingly. If we think in our present way, we will create the kind of world that we have created. If we think in another way, we might create a different world, and different people as well. Only the two together can change.

Q   Does a creator God also exist in your implicate order?

BOHM   The issue is not raised. I have an idea of an implicate order and beyond that a super-implicate order, and so on, to orders that are more and more subtle. I say there are many more subtle levels. The word "subtle" has a root subtext meaning "finely woven." You may think of nets of consciousness that are finer and finer, or we may think of capturing finer and finer aspects of the implicate order. This could go on indefinitely. Then it's up to the individual. I think there is an intelligence that is implicit there. A kind of intelligence unfolds. The source of intelligence is not necessarily in the brain. The ultimate source of intelligence is much more enfolded into the whole.

Now, as far as the question whether you want to call that "God," this depends on what you mean by the word, because taking it as a personal God might restrict it in some way. The suggestion is that there is something like life and mind enfolded in everything. If you carry that to the ultimate, then that might be what some of the religious people mean by the word "God." But the word "God" means many different things to different people, and it becomes hard to know exactly what is implied. The implicate order does not rule out God, nor does it say there is a God. But it would suggest that there is a creative intelligence underlying the whole, which might have as one of the essentials that which was meant by the word "God."

In this sense it says that any picture which we make through thought is limited, and even the idea of the implicate order is limited, although we hope it goes beyond previous limits. Only the ultimate is unlimited. However, as you say more about the unlimited you begin to limit it. If you say "The unlimited is God, and by God I mean this and this and this," then you begin to limit it. I think it is essential not to limit God, if you believe in God.

This was originally so in the Hebrew religion when they said the name of God is only "I am," and nothing more should be said. But they did not carry that out in a coherent way. I think it's essential to be coherent about it, otherwise it will tangle up. And to tangle up at this level is very destructive.

Q But you yourself were also searching for other frames of thinking. I'm touching now on your many encounters with Krishnamurti, for instance.

BOHM I got to know Krishnamurti in the early sixties. I became interested around that time in understanding the whole thing more deeply. I felt he was suggesting that it is possible for a human being to have some kind of contact with this whole. I don't think he would want to use the word "God" because of its limited associations.

Q Later you met also with the Dalai Lama. Did your ideas correspond with Tibetan Buddhism?

BOHM   What I want to do is to understand. I want to have a dialogue with different people to find out, to share how they are thinking: to participate. I feel that human thought tends to get over-focused and limit everybody to his own little area. It is important to be able to communicate and have a dialogue, to listen to each and everybody. Listening, and sharing these views, then perhaps we can go beyond them.

That is why I've talked with a great many people of different kinds, including the Dalai Lama. However, I think I had a much closer association with Krishnamurti because I was there for a long time with him until he died.

Q   Krishnamurti made the greatest impression on you?

BOHM   Yes. I felt that when I first saw him it opened up a tremendous area.

Now I think that there are certain similarities between what he says, and what the Buddha says, and what some others say. I was interested in pursuing all that.

The point about the Buddhist philosophy is that they have the notion of mutually dependent origination: everything originates together, mutually dependent. I think this is very close to the implicate order, which says that everything comes out of a ground and everything is interrelated, and that underlying it there is no substance that can be defined. That everything is mutually dependent also gives rise, I think, to what the Buddhists call the law of karma. But karma too becomes changeable since even our own state of mind is part of the whole, and when it changes, the whole changes, so the karma changes.

Q   I believe creativity is seen as a cornerstone of science for the first time through your thinking.

BOHM   I don't know if it is particularly in my thinking. I mean, many people have realized that creativity is an essential part of science. Creative insight is required for new steps. I feel that creativity is essential not only for science, but for the whole of life.

If you get stuck in a mechanical repetitious order, then you will degenerate. That is one of the problems that has grounded every civilization: a certain repetition. Then the creative energy gradually fades away, and that is why the civilization dies. Many civilizations vanished not only because of external pressure, but also because they decayed internally.

Q   Many people believe that creativity is always connected to the arts.

BOHM   It is connected to art, science, religion, but also to every aspect of life. I think that, fundamentally, all activity is an art. Science is a particular kind of art, which emphasizes certain things. Then we have the visual artists, the musical artists, and various kinds of other artists, who are specialized in different ways. But, fundamentally, art is present everywhere. The very word "art" in Latin means "to fit." The whole notion of the cosmos means "order" in Greek. It is an artistic concept really.

Q   Do you see a comparison between the shifts in contemporary art and the shifts in science?

BOHM   Yes, I think there is some similarity. The change began to occur at almost the same time, around the late nineteenth and early twentieth century. I think the first very plain indication of a change in the direction of art was the appearance of Impressionism, although it had been prepared before. You can say that the whole content of such painting is in spots of primary color. When you get closer it doesn't mean very much, but when you stand back at a certain distance suddenly a whole world emerges. I regard this as a kind of implicate order. The meaning of these spots of paint unfolds. The picture is enfolded in the spots.

I think there is a considerable similarity between that and how the mathematics of quantum theory works. Art is exploring fundamentally new modes of perception, through the senses, and new forms of imagination. And in so far as it does that it will be relevant to science and to spirituality.

I once saw a picture by Rouault of a clown. I think it was in the Edward G. Robinson Collection. The point was that there were all sorts of patches of color at the center of the clown, but there were complementary patches of color on the outside. Then I noticed the eye could move from one to the other, and the picture as a whole began to pulsate. And then suddenly there was a different vision, in which it seemed there was a circulation in the whole room, coming out of the clown and back to me. You see, it created another perception. It seems to me that artists can to some extent explore different forms of sense perception and the meaning of perception. You could say that Cézanne and the Cubists had a similar idea. Since then art has expanded in a very large number of directions, which are not very clear to me. Art began a new development then.

In the early days art was firmly tied to society by its various functions, such as representational pictures for religious purposes, and architecture, and making beautiful environments and various things. But all of that changed in the late nineteenth century. The connection between art and society became less important, and some artists began to explore new directions.

Q   If we see a connection between the arts, science, and spirituality, and we add to this the implicate order, could this influence future economic models?

BOHM   I think this question of economics requires some thought. I like to go into the roots of words, because they often show early insights, a fresh perception of meaning. The word "economy" has a Greek root, meaning "household management." The point is, what is the household? We can say there are so many households in the world and they all behave independently. In fact they are all interdependent. The earth is one household really, but we are not treating it that way. So the first step in economics is to say: "The earth is one household. It is all one."

The implicate order would help us to see that, to see that everything enfolds everything. To see that everybody not merely *depends* on everybody, but actually everybody *is* everybody in a deeper sense. We are the earth, because all our substance comes from the earth and goes back to it. It is a mistake to say it is an environment just surrounding us, because that would be like the brain regarding the rest of the body as part of its environment.

It is essential to see the world as one, because these households are not independent. The implicate order and all these similar ideas encourage you to see it as one. It is all mutual participation. Therefore you have to look at things that way. Now the question is, how do we manage this one household which is the world? But the first thing is to see that it is one. If we pretend it is many we cannot manage it.

Q   It seems that profit-making is now the big concern, but if you see the world as one household you would say that making profit is like stealing from your own pocket.

BOHM   If it is all one we must all stand or fall together. We have to find a way to do that. It is also politics, as well as economics, because we have all these separate governments. It can't work, you know. We need a new vision of the human being in the world. We now hope that the danger to the ecological balance will help bring that about.

Q  Could you give us a fundamental statement on your thinking on the whole, incorporating all these different aspects?

BOHM  Yes, first to focus on the question of seeing the whole coherently. It's not enough to have holism, it must also be coherent. Coherent means "to hang together." People may have incoherent views of the whole, which could be very destructive. In fact, some holistic theories have had very bad effects in the past. In a way, you could say the Nazis had a kind of holistic theory too. As I just said, it's not enough to have holism, although that too is important.

We must do justice to each of the parts, as well as understanding their relative independence, in order that there be freedom. The whole is not imposed, but is *in* each part and each part is in the whole. That is what I call participation. Currently that word has changed its meaning. It has two meanings now. One is "to partake of." We partake of the whole within ourselves. Another is "to take part in it actively." Both are necessary.

So this contrasts with the current atomistic view of society in which every person is an atom which just interacts externally. He does not partake of the whole. He is interacting only to get something for himself. The general view I have is that participation is fundamental. That means we must have dialogue. We must share our thoughts. We must be able to think together. If we can't think together and talk together, then we can do nothing together. But in fact that is the hardest thing in the world.

Q  What has given you the greatest satisfaction in your professional life?

BOHM  Well, I think that getting the implicate order was a great satisfaction, though I don't know if I could measure it as the greatest.

Q  What would you desire for the future of science?

BOHM  I would like to see it focusing more on quality than on precise quantitative mathematical concepts. I see the move towards the notion of participation as fundamental, rather than the atomistic analytic approach.

Q   And what would you desire for the future of mankind?

BOHM   The same thing really. I think that I would like to see mankind establish itself as one whole, with freedom for each of the parts, but with mutual participation; to come into a coherent whole, which would be creative.

Q   What are you doing at the moment?

BOHM   I am working with my colleague Dr. Basil Hiley on a book on physics.[1] I travel around a great deal. I lecture and we have seminars.

Q   Do you have the feeling that people are at last more sympathetic towards your ideas of the implicate order?

BOHM   People are picking up the ideas. It's more outside physics than inside physics. I think physicists seem to find it hard to see why you need the implicate order. The general attitude now is to give first priority for obtaining a set of equations that predict the results of experiments.

Q   People rely almost too much on mathematical models, even in economics.

BOHM   I feel that mathematics has been overemphasized in modern science. It does give a certain precision and so on, but at the cost of becoming a rather limited conceptual structure.

In the case of economics, I think this notion of mutual participation is crucial. Mathematics can understand this to some extent, as it does in the quantum theory, but I think basically we need to think of economics qualitatively, meaning we have a model in which we see that everything participates in everything. Therefore we don't have independent places and industries and substances. We don't think that a certain industry is just there in a certain place producing goods and then exchanging them with somebody else from somewhere else. Instead, the very existence of each group and the conditions for its existence are the result of factors that are unfolded from the whole earth.

I think you need this sort of way of thinking about it, but our current mathematics is too abstract to enable discussion of such things. It is so abstract that people lose sight of the concrete reality. They make a calculation, which is always an abstraction, *and then fail to see from which point it is abstracted*. I think mathematics can provide some backup to make more precision possible, but only on the basis of having this qualitative understanding beforehand.

You see, in times past this qualitative culture existed, although it had certain inadequacies too. Mathematics helped to unlock a great deal of technological progress, but it also created vast numbers of problems which we still don't know how to solve.

Q   What does the word "culture" mean to you?

BOHM   It is relevant to consider culture. Culture implies shared meaning, in which everybody participates. Culture is inherently a participatory thing. Our present culture is not at all coherent. It's highly incoherent all over the world and in each country. We need a coherent culture. In fact, we could say that one of the reasons why we have to enter into dialogue is to establish this coherent culture.

At present people cannot really talk with each other freely. For example, in the United Nations they talk only about a few small points which are negotiable, but most of the basic issues are not negotiable. Therefore they cannot really talk about the real problems.

We need to look at all our problems as negotiable and in that way create a common culture. But everybody has a different meaning now. In the East, for example, the professed meaning has been primarily to put the collective welfare first. In the West we profess to put the individual first. Neither culture does what it professes very well, but still that is what is professed. As long as these two approaches are not negotiable, we really can't get together and have a common culture. We have got to be able to really listen to each other and work through all this, and perhaps come to a new culture that is not limited by those two positions.

Q   What does it mean to you to bring art, science, and spirituality together?

BOHM   I think it is a step towards establishing a common culture. Science, art, and spirituality have been the basic features of culture all through the ages. We could also add technology as a development from science. If you put those three together you could say there is not a lot of culture that is not included in these three. It would be a big step to be able to have a coherent culture involving these three.

Q   Do you feel optimistic about such a development?

BOHM   Well, I have an attitude that I call "tactical optimism." I assume that it can be done. I see no reason why it can't be done. It may be difficult, but I think we must begin by assuming it can be done. We must start to establish a coherent meaning for the whole. But the key, the start, is to be able to have a dialogue. That way people in different groups can dialogue and really share their meanings, and perhaps emerge with new meanings.

For example, I would like to suggest—this is a fantasy of mine—a dialogue of scientists. I think scientists are among the people who would find it the hardest to dialogue, because each one thinks he knows the truth. But we don't have to go through all that. If we find the right people who are open enough in all areas we can start the dialogue. We should have a place where people can get together merely to talk without trying to solve any problem, but simply to communicate, just simply to share, and to see if they can come to a common understanding.

Q    I want to take you back to one other question. The three-dimensional model has been broken by artists, but also by other people, and it has provided us with a multidimensional view. First we had a universe, now we have a multiverse.

BOHM    Yes, I think that the implicate order implies a multidimensional view, in that we have a vast dimensionality, a much richer sort of reality. One of the interesting questions is how, from the point of view of physics, the implicate order with its many dimensions condenses down to the three-dimensional order, and the ordinary level of experience. That is the question which my colleague Basil Hiley and I are very interested in exploring mathematically.

Q    In addition to science, multidimensionality has also entered art and spirituality.

BOHM    I think in art the multidimensional order first appeared clearly with Impressionism, and then on from Cubism. The "spirit," too, must be regarded as multidimensional. It can't exist on one line.

I think that we must have a way of thinking and perceiving which brings everything together. What is common to all three basic attitudes is the question of thought. They all involve thought. Now, one of the ways in which thought has developed is in a direction which I call *literal*.

By this I mean that it aims to give a literal representation of reality as it actually is. It is maybe admitted that it is incomplete or not entirely correct, but that is nevertheless what we aim at. I think that this is a very limited sort of thought. What is left out is that thought is participatory, that thought has produced everything that we see here in our society. Wherever you look is the product of thought: buildings, farms, airplanes, everything, including pollution.

But not only that—thought also produces and shapes our perception of reality. We see reality according to our thought. Therefore thought is constantly participating both in giving shape and form and figuration to ourselves, and to the whole of reality. Now, thought doesn't know this. Thought is thinking that it isn't doing anything. I think this is really where the difficulty is. We have got to see that thought is part of this reality and that we are not merely *thinking about it*, but that we are *thinking it*. Do you see the difference?

Q  I agree with you, but why is it so difficult to get this into practice? Why is the task of the thinkers, and also of the scientists, so limited?

BOHM  The difficulty is, first of all, fragmentation. Everybody and every thought is broken up into bits, like this nation, this country, this region, this profession, and so on. It is extremely hard to break into that. But that comes about primarily because thought has developed traditionally in such a way that it claims not to be affecting anything, just telling you the way things are. Therefore people cannot see that they are creating a problem and are then apparently trying to solve it.

Let's take a problem. What problem do you like? Pollution? Ecology is not in itself a problem. It works perfectly well by itself. It becomes a problem because we are thinking in a certain way, by breaking everything up, and with each person doing his own thing. Therefore the ecological problem is due to the way we think. Thought thinks pollution is a problem "out there" and it must solve it. Now that doesn't make sense because simultaneously thought is creating all of the activities which make the problem in the first place and then creates another set of activities to try to overcome it.

Thought doesn't stop doing the things which are making the ecological problem, or the national problem, or whatever the problem is. Now, I think that is really why it is so hard to put a new consciousness into practice, because we are unconsciously in our practice doing the opposite of what we claim we want to do. Therefore the important point is to be aware of what we are actually doing.

Q   How would you suggest to spread this awareness among people, to make it understood and put into practice? Do we start at school, in the university?

BOHM   It would be a mistake to try to put it into practice. That is already a contradiction. As I said before, we have begun by doing one thing, we keep on doing it, and we try by means of a practice to overcome what we are doing in the opposite direction. That is like somebody who is hitting himself with his right hand trying to stop it with his left hand. The basic difficulty is that our practice is unaware of the fact that it is producing all these problems.

I think we need another approach, which is: we have got to be aware of what is going on. Take for example the difficulty of communication. There is no practice which will establish communication, except communicating itself, and encountering the problems of communicating. If people want to communicate, and if we say we have got a practical problem, this is going to limit us. So suppose we say "We want to communicate," *but we are not going to set up a problem*. A long time ago I read about an anthropologist who studied some North American Indians of quite a primitive stage. From time to time they would get around in a circle, everybody, and just talk and talk and talk, as equals. They made no decisions on anything, and at some point they just stopped. Then everybody seemed to know what to do. By doing this constantly they understood each other so well that it wasn't very hard to know what to practice.

Now, we can't do that. Imagine people all getting together. Even in one country they can't do it, or in one family, much less between countries and cultures and religions. If you ask what practice can we get by which we can start to do this, it is not going to make sense, because we're saying unconsciously that we are committed to doing just the opposite. Then we will try to overcome it; that is as if we are forever unconsciously resisting the very thing we are trying to do.

Q   It's in the human being itself.

BOHM   Yes, it is in his memory and in his background and in his whole system, and also in the culture.

Q   So do we have to accept that?

BOHM   I think we have to transform the culture, by beginning with a nucleus which makes a new culture. It doesn't begin with a practice. *Practice must follow out of something deeper.* It really shouldn't follow out of a decision to carry out a practice, but rather by common perception of the need to do something. When people start to do that, then they can work on it. If everybody understands the same thing and has the same end in view, they will work together. But if everybody has a different end in view they are going to be at cross-purposes and it will not work. I think the real trouble is that we don't have a coherent culture. Perhaps in earlier times primitive people did have such a coherent culture. At least one can choose to believe that, though I don't know for sure. One of the first steps is for people to engage in dialogue together, without trying to solve any problem, you see.

Q   But do you believe that mankind will come that far, that we will establish a common coherent culture together?

BOHM   I think it is essential. If we can't, then I don't think the human race is viable at more than the level of the Stone Age. With the arrival of modern technology we have to take this step, or we can't go on.

Q   Who will listen?

BOHM   Some people will listen. It will begin with those who will listen, and a certain number are ready to listen. They are the nucleus. We could call this the micro-culture, the micro-cosm of the bigger culture. You see, if we could establish a micro-culture, this could then spread. That's the suggestion. I don't think we can establish it as an end in view, because that end is already distorted by all the unconscious motives, and also by resistance. For example, people tried to establish socialism but all the unconscious motives of self-centered-ness resisted it, it never really worked.

Q   Exploring the mind and getting more of a hold on the mind is probably creating a future that could be quite different, because the motivation changes.

BOHM   Well, that would certainly change the culture and the society. What we need is to be able to talk, to communicate. At present there are great differences and many of these are not negotiable. What is needed is a dialogue in the real sense of the word "dialogue," which means "flowing through," amongst people, rather than an exchange like a game of ping-pong. The word "discussion" really means "to break up everything," to analyze and have an exchange, like a game. Therefore, we need this dialogue; the spirit of the dialogue is not competition, but it means that if we find something new, then everybody wins.

The basic idea of this dialogue is to be able to talk while suspending your opinions, holding them in front of you, while neither suppressing them nor insisting upon them. Not trying to convince, but simply to understand. The first thing is that we must perceive all the meanings of everybody together, without having to make any decisions or saying who's right and who's wrong. It is more important that we all see the same thing. That will create a new frame of mind in which there is a common consciousness. It is a kind of implicate order, where each one enfolds the whole consciousness. With the common consciousness we then have something new—a new kind of intelligence.

## NOTE

1   See Bohm, D. and Hiley, B. J. (1993) *The Undivided Universe*. London: Routledge.

# BIBLIOGRAPHY

Bohm, D. (1951) *Quantum Theory*. New York: Dover.
—— (1965, 1996) *The Special Theory of Relativity*. London: Routledge.
—— (1980) *Wholeness and the Implicate Order*. London: Routledge.
—— (1992, 1994) *Thought as a System*. London: Routledge.
—— (1996) *On Dialogue*. London: Routledge.
—— and Hiley, B. J. (1993) *The Undivided Universe*. London: Routledge.
Field, J. (1936, 1981) *A Life of One's Own*. Los Angeles: Jeremy Tarcher.
Rosenthal, M. (1996) *Abstraction in the Twentieth Century: Total Risk, Freedom, Discipline*. New York: Guggenheim Museum Publications.

# INDEX

abstraction 76; in art 35;
   mathematics as 112; particles as
   75, 91; self as 99–100, 100–1
aesthetic perception 47
Archimedes 15
architects 17
art 109; abstraction in 35; action of
   nature as 89–90; as assimilation
   of nature 28; change in
   direction of 110; definition 81,
   109; differences between
   science and 32; factual aspect of
   38; and feelings 37; historical
   development 35; in life as a
   whole 86; link with science
   through beauty 31–2, 33;
   mathematics as form of 82, 83;
   as morally neutral 87, 88; and
   multidimensionality 114;
   objectivity of 28, 37–8; as
   paradigm structures 34, 35;
   reasoning as 84–5; in relation to
   "fitting" 85, 86–7; in relation to
   "the good" 86–7; and religion
   29; science as 82, 84–6; self-
   knowledge 30; separation
   between science and 31, 80;
   similarity between shifts in
   science and shifts in 109;
   structure in 35–6, 38; unity with
   science 36–7
artamovement 91–3
artistic spirit 30, 37, 104
assimilation 27–8, 30, 32, 37
atoms 48–9, 74, 76, 90, 99

attention: as basis for creativity
   25–6; movement of 79; and
   symbolic function of language
   68, 94–5; truth and the ordering
   of 94; on world views 73
axiomatic approach 34, 53, 54
awareness 115–16

Barfield, Owen 41, 42
beauty 17; definition 81, 87; as
   harmony of order 11; and laws
   of universe 31; link between
   science and art through
   31–2, 33
biology 90
Bohr, Niels 102, 103, 104
Bondo, Professor Hermann 32
Brownian motion 8, 9–10
Buddhism 108

Cézanne, Paul 35, 109
children: and learning 3–4 , 5, 16;
   and mechanical orders 19–20;
   thought 56–7, 66, 68
Coleridge, Samuel 41–2, 46, 50, 53,
   54, 55, 56
common consciousness 118
communication 65, 116
concept 5, 16
conformity 16–17
confusion 22; and disorder 21; and
   neurosis 21; self-sustaining
   21–2, 25; simple 21
consciousness 106, 115–16;
   common 118

120